Sanskrit and Related Studies

Sri Garib Dass Oriental Series – No.84

Sanskrit and Related Studies

Contemporary Researches and Reflections

Editors :-
Bimal Krishna Matilal
&
Purusottama Bilimoria

SRI SATGURU PUBLICATIONS
a Division of
Indian Books Centre
Delhi–India.

Published by :–
Sri Satguru Publications,
Indological and Oriental Publishers
A Division of
Indian Books Centre,
40/5, Shakti Nagar,
Delhi–110 007
India.

First Edition — Delhi, 1990.

ISBN–81–7030–192–0

Printed in India at
IMH PRESS Pvt. Ltd.
A - 48 Kailash Colony
New Delhi - 110048

To the

Sacred Memory of

Gopal Bhattacharyya

Contents

Preface

The papers brought together in this volume were presented at a conference on Sanskrit and Contemporary Research in 1983, to coincide with the Indian Festive and Cultural Celebrations that were then taking place in New York. The conference was organized by the late Professor Gopal Bhattacharyya during his short tenure, towards the last years of his life, at State University of New York's College at New Paltz in New York. This volume is dedicated to the memory of Gopal Bhattacharyya; hence we feel it is proper to say something about the life and career of the scholar to whose efforts indeed this collection is owed.

Gopal Bhattacharyya was borne in 1915 in Bengal into a family of Sanskrit scholars. His undergraduate education was at Calcutta University, and later, in his more years, he went to Melbourne, Australia, to complete a Master of Education degree (1955-1962). But in 1948, following the assassination of Mahatma Gandhi, Mr Bhattacharyya joined the Gandhian Basic Training Scheme in Wardha, Madhya Pradesh. There he embraced the Gandhian model of teaching moral values and vocational training which he put into practice at a tribal school in Campaknagar, Tripura. Later he was to be the principal of the teachers' training college in Agartala, Tripura.

Drawn also to the kindred spiritual thoughts of Sri Aurobindo, Mr Bhattacharyya became active in the local Sri Aurobindo Centre, and he was a life-long member of the Sri Aurobindo Society. This interest took him, in 1969, to Matagiri, a community centre in upstate New York, devoted to furthering the ideals of Sri Aurobindo. There he had started to hold classes in Sanskrit; and shortly afterwards he took up a post at the College at New Paltz teaching Sanskrit and Indian philosophy. Mr Bhattacharyya retired from the college soon after the successful Sanskrit conference and moved to West Cultural Centre. He took ill and died there on June 6, 1985. And although, Mr Bhattacharyya had made plans to publish this collection the task remained unaccomplished.

The editors would like to acknowledge their gratitude to the members of Mr Bhattacharyya's family, in particular Dr. Ajit Bhattacharyya, for their support in bringing out this publication, and also to IMH Press and the Indian Books Centre, in seeing this volume though press. Last but not least, we would like to thanks the authors whose articles are inclnded herein, for their ready co-operation and long patience.

R K M (Oxford)
P B (Victoria)

Section A
Sanskrit Language and Linguistics

1

On Bhartṛhari's Linguistic Insight

BIMAL KRISHNA MATILAL

I

Bhartṛhari, the fifth-century grammarian-philosopher of India, propounded the thesis that verbalizability (or, verbal or linguistic activity at some implicit level) is immanent in our cognitive faculty (VP. I, verses 123-124). In fact, it is claimed that the cognitive faculty operates necessarily with the verbal faculty. Speech or language is not just an inessential but convenient conveyor belt of thought; rather it constitutes its vital part. This does not mean that we always make audible noises with our vocal chord whenever we cognize, think or perceive anything. Nor is it proper to say that we make 'inaudible' noise as we are aware of things or facts. On the other hand, it implies that we verbalize at some *deeper* level as we cognize and we cognize as we verbalize. To put it bluntly, a cognition does not COGNIZE if it does not verbalize, at least, at some implicit level. The question is : how are we supposed to understand this thesis?

If Bhartṛhari is right then it is proper to claim that a so-called private and subjective cognitive event is equivalent to the occurrence of a verbal thought, and if a thought is verbalized, that is, expressed in language, it breaks through the 'privacy' enclosure and becomes a *public* property that is communicable and inter-subjectively available. What happens to one's private sensory experience or sensation? A tentative answer from Bhartṛhari's point of view would be this: As soon as the sensory reaction stops being simply a physical or physiological event and matures into a sensory awareness, as soon as it penetrates into the cognitive level, it becomes pregnant with WORD,

SABDA, or verbalizability. But this is, perhaps, putting the thesis too strongly.

Let us consider two versions of the Bhartṛhari thesis, the strong and the week. The strong thesis is:

B1 : All cognitive episodes are equivalent to verbal thoughts.

This will exclude many primitive, pre-linguistic, non-verbal experiences from the domain of awareness-episode and declare them to be non-cognitive in character. It is somewhat doubtful whether Bhartṛhari intended his thesis in this form. A weaker version will allow, however, for certain primitive, pre-linguistic, cognitive episodes among which we can put the so-called pure sensory experience, "raw feels" etc. The weaker version is:

B2 : Most cognitive episodes are verbal thoughts at some implicit level.

However, the argument cited to make B1 seems plausible is the following (VP.I, verse 124) : The revelatory or illuminative power of consciousness is necessarily interwined with *vāg-rūpatā*, the power of articulating the grasped object in language. This power is *natural* to awareness. Since an awareness-episode has to reveal *(prakāśa)* some object or other, it has to contain the *seed* of verbalization or verbal discrimination *(vimarśa)*.

I shall quote a few sentences from the *Vṛtti*-sentences which cannot be easily made sense of. The difficulty of the style of the *Vṛtti* is well-known and sometimes baffling. Since K. A. Subrahmania Iyer translated the *Vṛtti*, I have chosen only one or two cases where Iyer's translation is not very clear, if not entirely misleading. To make my point clear, I shall attempt at some sort of explanatory translation, and this will make my minimal differences form Iyer's interpretation obvious.

II

Text 1 : Just as the *Śabdabhāvanā* (residual traces of linguistic ability) where explicit forms are withdrawn *(samhṛtarūpā)* cannot accomplish anything *(kāryam na kriyate)*, similarly the non-conceptual *(a-vikalpaka)* cognition is of no use.

Text 2 : (This is the most baffling sentence. I shall divide it into 5 parts). (a) For example, when one walks quickly and touches grass and pebbles, a (tactile) awareness arises. (b) But even though such an awareness arises *(saty api jñāne)* that is indeed a unique or a vague *(kācid eva)* state of cognition in which *(yasyām)* an object's nature *(vastvātmā)* is said to be cognized *(jñāyate ity abhidhīyate)* provided the object is tinged with awareness *(jñānāugata)* and its explicit form shines forth *(vyaktarūpapratyāvabhāsa)*. (c) This state (of cognition) contains the ready or about-to-sprout *(abhimukhībhūta)* seed of the residual traces of Language *(śabdabhāvanābīja)*. (d) There are two types of words, articulate words that are speakable and the non-articulate that are unspeakable *(ākhyeyarūpāṇām anākheyarūpāṇām ca śabdānām)* [I take the inarticulate words refer to the linguistic ability of the babies, for they act to suck their mother's breasts, etc. being prompted by such word-impregnated awareness cf. *anākheya-śabda-nibandhanā bālānām pravṛttiḥ, Vṛtti* on verse 113]. (e) And there arises denotative power of the words regulated by each denotatum *(pratyarthaniyatāsu śaktiṣu)* while the object is picked out *(upagṛhyamāna)* and given a form *(ākriyamāṇa)* by that cognition which is impregnated with words *(śabdānuviddhena)* and empowered with that denotative power (common to the words) *(śaktyanupātinā)*.

Text 3 : Speech *(vāc)* indwells or inheres in all cases of awareness just as illumination does in fire and consciousness in the mind *(antaryāmin)*. The subtle nature of *Vāc* (speech) [i.e., *sūkṣmo vāgdharmaḥ*] penetrates and permeates even such states as lack ostensible mental activity *(asañcetitāvasthā)*. Even the epistemologically first-born *(prathamopanipātin)* illumination *(prakāśa)* of the external objects (bāhyārtha), since it cannot apprehend the *nimitta* or the special features that cause our usage of certain words (to denote the object, such as 'white', 'cow'), make the self-same object *(vastu-*

svarūpamātra) appear in our awareness *(pratyavabhāsayati)* by some unspecifiable designation such as 'this' or 'that' *(idam tad ity avapadeśyayā vṛttyā).*

III

These passages give an outline of a theory which has been variously defended and argued in many places of the *Kārikas* and the *Vṛtti*. Utpaladeva and Abhinavagupta, proponents of the Kāśmir Saivaite school, assimilated this theory into their metaphysical doctrine of Śiva-consciousness, although they supported what is called *śabdādhyāsa-vāda* as opposed to Bhartṛhari's *śabdādvaita-vāda*. I shall use the remarks of Utpala and Abhinava to expound further the thesis of the language-impregnated nature of awareness. For it has some important implications for the theories of perceptual awareness.

Most Indian philosophers, the Buddhist, the Naiyāyikas, and the Mimāṃsakas, have argued for ages that there are two types of perceptual awareness, *nirvikalpa* and *savikalpa*, and by almost common consent the first is the sensory awareness where no concept and hence no language or word *(śabda)* can appear, and the second is one where words, concepts and universals are essentially present. The usual arguments is that the epistemologically first-born has to do only with the *pure* object, the given, where *śabda* has no place, and the clearest examples are supposedly the baby's "raw feels", the mute's awareness etc. Bhartṛhari and following him Utpala and Abhinava maintained the opposite view; viz., that even the so-called *nirvikalpa* state, the awareness is interpenetrated with *śabda* or *vāg-rūpatā*. For, it is argued, without such *vāg-rūpatā* which Bhartṛhari calls *pratyavamarśa* (1, verse 124) and the Kāśmiris call *vimarśa*, sometimes *parāmarśa*, an awareness cannot be aware of an object, illumination will not illuminate *(na prakāśaḥ prakāśeta)* !

This theory of cognition claims that there are two inherent, inalienable, mutually complementary powers or properties of any awareness-episode, *prakāśa* and *vimarśa*. For lack of any convenient English terms, let us call them, "illumination" and "discrimination." Now, 'illumination' means removal of darkness but simple removal of darkness does not reveal unless one is able to *distinguish* the outline of the object from its immediate surroundings or environment. Throwing a flood of light upon a canvas is only half of the whole process of showing the object, the picture of the object must be sufficiently distinguished from the background to make it visible. If *prakāśa* is the flood of light, *vimarśa* is what makes the object distinguishable and distinct. An awareness is thus both *prakāśa* and *vimarśa* or to use a modern Wittgensteinian jargon, an awareness is both *showing* and *saying*. The so-called per-linguistic grasp of the object cannot have any firm grip unless the object is sufficiently distinguished, and if it is sufficiently distinguished, *vimarśa* has already set in, and a *śabda-bhāvanā* is implicit. A pure *prakāśa* without *vimarśa* is impossible in this theory. In fact, it is not, even like saying with a modern philosopher like Immanul Kant or Nelson Goodman that perception without conception is mute and conception without perception is blind. It is rather like saying: Perception without conception is blind and conception without perception is mute.

Some empirical arguments have been cited in favour of this not too obvious thesis. Bhartṛhari has said that even a newborn baby acts, cries, sucks mother's breast etc. by virtue of an awareness where the seed of *śabdabhāvanā* must have been sown. Implicit in such argument are a special theory of action, of awareness and their inter-relationship. All our activities are implicitly prompted by some specific awareness of some purpose or other. The instinctual awareness of the babies, awareness that prompts them to act, to cry and even to make effort to articulate the first words, must be a sort of awareness where the purpose and the method to achieve the purpose are distinguished and it presupposes *vimarśa* and hence *śabdabhāvanā*.

Critics, mainly the Buddhists but the Naiyāyikas and Mīmāṃsakas as well, would strongly disapprove of the above thesis of Bhartṛhari. I shall, therefore, supplement Bhartṛhari's arguments with those suggested by Utpala and Abhinava. Utpala says that the very nature *(svabhāva)* of illumination *(avabhāsa-prakaśa)* is *vimarśa* as it has been recognized by others (such as Bhartṛhari), for otherwise cognitive illumination would be as inert, material and passive as *jaḍa* object, a crystal or a mirror, for example (IP, 1.5.11). In IP, 1.5.19, Utpala says that even in sensory awareness *(sākṣātkāra)* there is *vimarśa*, for otherwise how the instantaneous running would have been possible (by seeing a snake, for example) for someone who not has done any *pratisandhāna*. This *pratisandhāna* is a form of *vimarśa* and can be articulated as a consideration *(paramarśa)* of the form: 'this is dangerous', 'I must act quickly' etc., etc. Abhinava says about *anusandhāna* or *pratisandhāna: idam iṣṭam idam iṣyate, idaṃ ca eṣaṇīyam iti hānopādānecchā anusamdhānena upalakṣitam* (IPV. P. 233, II). ("This is desired", "this will be desired", and "this is desirable" — such desire to obtain or to avoid is indicated by the word "anusandhāna").

Abhinava formulates the following argument to explain Utpala: In our instantaneous running, speaking etc., our preceding perception cannot be differentiated or separated from volitional element, for otherwise there would not be that immediacy or instantaneousness. For if volition follows consideration which follows perceptual grasp, there would certainly be a delayed action. Now, a volitional element necessitates the fact that *vimarśa* is present in such perception because *vimarśa* always regulates the volition and volitional element in turn regulates the (motivated) action.

Abhinava elaborately discusses the relevant criticisms of his opponents represented mainly by Dharmakīrti who would reject any possibility of *vimarśa, vikalpa or śabda*, in contaminating the purity of *nirvikalpa*, sensory awareness, I shall give only a synopsis of Abhinava's detailed analysis of Dharmakīrti's argument. First, Dharmakīrti would argue that the object that flashes in our awareness (*pratibhāsate, gṛhyate)* is not identical with the object that is determined or ascertained by *śabda (adhyavasīyate, vimṛśyate)*, and hence the sensory perception cannot coincide with *vikapla* or word-impregnated awareness or construction. Several points are raised to support this issue of the ultimate separation of what is apprehensible (*grāhya* or *pratibhāsamāna*) and what is determinable or distinguishable by word (*adhyavaseya*). For example, in PV III, 194, ff, it is said that sense perception arises from the capacity of the object (*arthaśamarthya*) whereas the word-impregnated awareness is given by the following sequence: sensation leading to the awakening of a *saṃskara* (disposition to remember), leading to the remembering to the *saṃketa*, (the relevant word) leading finally to *vikalpa* or *śabda-yojanā* (articulation of awareness in words). Abhinava comments with a touch of irony that the sensory perception is in this way like the great-grandfather of *vikalpa*. Of these the Buddhist would agree to eliminate the third element, for awakening of *Saṃskāra* would be enough for the *śabdayojanā* to arise.

In reply to this thesis of ultimate separation *grāhya* and *adhyavaseya*, both Utpala and Abhinava say that this is contradicted by the 'self-awareness' (*sva-samvedana*) doctrine of the Buddhists themselves. For each awareness is said to be aware of itself and hence in a perception which is self-aware both what is revealed or apprehended *(pratibhāsamāna)* and what is determined or ascertained (*adhyavaseya*) must be the self-same awareness. As regards the above point about *śabdayojanā* being delayed by its necessary casual condition, it is said by Abhinava that *śabdayojanā* might have other causal conditions, and hence it may not always arise from the remembering of the *saṃketa* (convention). In fact Utpala and Abhinava say that the kind of *śabdayojanā* that is needed in the epistemologically first perception, can arise from what is called *manaskāra* mental attention, which, the Buddhist agrees, is associated with perception. The *Abhidharma* says that the concept *manaskāra* means *cittābhoga*, 'expansion of the mind'. *Manaskāra* is also the fixation of the (usually fleeting) mind, (*avahitatvalakṣaṇa*). In the casual conditions of a perceptual awareness, mental attention or *manaskāra* is to be included side by side with the faultlessness of the eye organs, non-dimness of light and placing of the object at a proper distance. Here, Abhinava says, just as the object accounts for the *pratibhāsa* 'appearance' of the object in the awareness, the *manaskāra* mental attention accounts for the *vimarśa* 'distinguishing' of the same, resulting in a full fledged perceptual awareness. In fact, *manaskāra* 'mental attention' is defined by Abhinava as the readiness for *vimarśa* distinguishing' *(cf. vimarśonmukhatā)*. In this way, the two aspects of perception, the apprehensible and the determinable, *(prakāśa and vimarśa)* are not incompatible with each other and hence can arise together because (and when) either has its own causal antecedent present at the same time. The *manaskāra* (mental attention impregnates the perception with *subtle* word seeds, and this is called the *pratisamhṛta-rūpa-śabda-yojanā* a very 'contracted' or 'primitive form of ascertainment through words' or 'an ascertainment through words withdrawn to themselves'. For such *śabda-yojanā*, (ascertainment through words), a prior *saṃketa* is not needed.

The Buddhist points out that the child's first perception cannot be thus impregnated with the word-seed, for the child does not have even the *saṃketa*. Abhinava says that even the child's first perception cannot be completely innocent of *vimarśa*, for otherwise it would be impossible to explain satisfactorily his attempt to articulate a word through vocal organ and to learn a *saṃketa*. A *saṃketa-grahaṇa* takes the following form: looking at a cow the child learns to use the word "cow" from such instruction: "This is a cow" or "This is called a cow". Here ascription of the word or even the predicate cow would be impossible unless there is a presentation of the subject by *vimarśa* or *paramarśa* (*determination*). For the presentation of the subject in the sentence the speaker used "this", and this is clearly a *vimarśa*. The child also cognises the subject by some similar *vimarśa* — an implicitly word-impregnated awareness. Explicit use of word is not necessary, as it has been already emphasized. Even the pointing of the finger, nodding of the head, would represent *vimarśa*, word-impregnated awareness. Abhinava says that sometimes we clearly learn the *saṃketa* of a word where the object is identified by another word: 'A cuckoo is called *pika* ", "A cat is called pussy", and so on. From this we can generalize that when we learn even the *saṃketa* of the first word in our life, the subject is also identified, i.e., discriminated for us, by some *vimarśa* where the word-seed is present, and such *vimarśa* is made possible not by a prior learning of *saṃketa* but by what has been called *manaskāra* (mental attention).

The situation is sometimes reminiscent of the nativist theory in the Western tradition. In a way it also smacks of the Socratic quip: Learning is but remembering. But it is more important to understand the emphasis that this theory puts elsewhere: the particular nature of the cognitive activity. *Manaskāra* is an essential causal condition of each cognitive awareness, and since the child's sensory perception is also cognitive in nature, the sense-object or the sense-given must also be sufficiently differentiated to be tinged with *vimarśa* or *vikapla* or *śabdanā*, if not with the usual word, say "a cow", with a least, 'this' or that.

Dharmakirti has said (PV) that when we suspend all our *cintā* 'thinking' and when the inner faculty is inert, the eye would be able to see the object but no *vimarśa* would be possible at that stage. Abhinava says in reply that this state (when all thoughts are suspended) cannot be followed by an *adhyavasāya* under usual circumstances for in the immediately preceding moment there is no *manaskāra* or *cintā*. And if so, then it would be impossible to establish that such a state existed. We cannot even remember it, for the seed of the memory has not been sown by *vimarśa* (mental attention). And if we would remember it, or if the *vimarśa* or *adhyavasāya* follows then we have to say that thought (*cintā*) was not totally suspended, for it was somehow infected with *vimarśa*. Hence it is established : Since each sensory awareness is causally preceded by *manaskāra* and since it is also aware of itself, we cannot deny that besides perceiving or seeing, the state of sensory awareness must be performing the other too, *vimarśa* or *śabdanā* (IPV, P 238).

In spite of the above, Abhinava says we can still talk about a *nirvikalpa-savikapla* distinction in this theory. When *śabdabhāvanā* is *saṃvṛta*, contracted or withdrawn into itself, we can call the state *nirvikapla* compared to another state where *śabdabhāvanā* is *prasārita* 'expanded' or 'blown up' (which is *sa-vikalpa*).

Let us note that this theory is not simply repeating a platitude. For instance, some of us may feel that we cannot think without words, for thought is after all in Plato's language, the "inner dialogue" of the soul. A modern philosopher, D. Davidson, has said that this platitude is of a piece with "primitive behaviorism" which being "baffled by the privacy of unspoken thought may take comfort in the view that thinking is really 'talking to oneself', 'silent speech.' This platitude, it had been argued by Davidson and Quine, wrongly leads us to believe that since of thought and language, language may be easier to understand, it should have the privileged position over thought in our study. But indeed, language and thought, are only two sides of the same coin. Davidson says, "The two are indeed linked in the sense that each requires the other in order to be understood. "For Bhartṛhari, this linkage is also essential and fundamental like that between *prakāśa* and *vimarśa.*

Some philosophers today avoid the epistemologist's dilemma by claiming that even a pure sensory datum is elusive unless it is re-inforced by language (Wittgenstein). In Quine's expression, the point is that this is how public language anchors experience arresting drift. But Bhartṛhari's claim seems to be even more fundamental. Here both language anchors experience and experience anchors language. Of modern philosophers,W. Sellars had put the point in the strongest language with regard to abstract entities:

> Of all awareness of *sort, resembles, facts* etc.—in short, all awareness of abstract entities—indeed all awareness even of particulars—is a linguistic affair.

For Bhartṛhari's holism, all entities, even particulars, bits and pieces of matter, are all abstracts, for they are abstracted from the *whole*, and it is no wonder that they are a sort of linguistic affair, being generated by the word-impregnated awareness of *vimarśa* or *vikalpa.*

NOTES AND REFERENCES

Abhinavagupta, (IP) : *Īśvarapratyabhijñāvimarśinī*, vols. I-III ed. M. K. Shastri, Kashmir Studies and Text Series, Srinagar, 1938, 1941, 1943.

Bhartṛhari (VP) *Vākyapadīya*

(i) eds. K. V. Abhyankar and V. P. Limaye, Poona, University, 1965.

(ii) *Kāṇda I*, ed. K. A. Subramania Iyer, Poona, Deccan College, 1966.

(iii) *Kāṇda* III, Part I, with Helārāja's commentary, ed. K. A. Subramania Iyer, Poona, Deccan College, 1963.

Davidson, D. Thought and Talk, in *Mind and Language* ed. S. D. Guttenplan, Oxford, 1975.

Dharmakīrti (PV). *Pramāṇavārttika* ed. Swami Dwarikadas Sastri, Varanasi, Bauddha-Bharati, 1968.

Goodman, N. *Ways of Wordmaking*, Sussex, Harvester Press, 1978.

Kant, I. *the Critique of Pure Reason*, trans. Norman Kemp Smith, London, Macmillan, 1958.

Sellars, W. *Science Perception and Reality*, London, Kegan Paul, 1963.

2

The Negative A-/ An- Prefix in Sanskrit

ALEX WAYMAN

For translation of philosophical and other type texts of India, there is a critical issue : the translation of negatives. The negatives are found in several forms in Sanskrit. There is a particle of prohibition or negation, *mā*. The nominal and verbal prefixes *vi*- and *nis*- (also *niḥ*- and *nir*-) have a range of usage including the cases when they are negative or privative, prevalently with the significance 'without'. Besides, Pāṇini, *Aṣṭa*, II, 3, 32,[1] shows that the words *pṛthak, vinā* and, *nānā* all mean 'without'; but by usage these words have different meanings of 'not being together', thus *pṛthagjana* ('separate person') *vinā* ('deprived of'), *nānā*- ('of different kinds', hence 'manifold'). The post-position word *ṛte* also means 'without' in the sense of 'except for'. The preposition *ni*- meaning 'down' is perhaps the *ni*- of the old words *ny-arṇa* ('waterless') and *ṅy-artha* ('going amiss, failure'), as well as of *ny-ahna* ('the closing day').

The topic of the present paper is the negative particle *na*, for which Pāṇini uses the reference *nañ*. The grammars must tell the cases when the *n* of the negative particle is elided, when in the latter case an augment is added — in fact also *n*; and those cases when the negative particle remains unchanged. Pāṇini, VI, 3, 73 mentions the general case, that *n* of the negative participle *nañ* is elided when it is the first member of a compound; and VI, 3, 74; when the *n* is elided, the augment of *n* is added to a word beginning with a vowel.[2] Hence, these are the two cases of negative *a*- / *an*- prefix. The *Vārttika* on this : It is also elided when the second member is a verb, provided censure is implied, for example : *apacasi tvaṃ jālma* ("Thou cookest not, O Knave"). The grammarians claim six senses for a 'compound' of which it is the first member.[3] Pāṇṇi,II, 2, 6 : the final member is inflected and it is a Tatpuruṣa compound.[4]

Pāṇṇi,VI, 3, 75,[5] gives a list of words for which the negative particle remains unchanged, among which a few are probably false etymologies, for example *napāt* (cognate with 'nephew') and *nakṣatra* (probably from *nakṣ-*), and also others that are undoubtedly valid compounds, e.g. *napuṃsaka* ('not male'). VI, 3, 76 gives the rule that the negative particle remains unchanged with *eka* which has the ablative augment *ad* (in numerals), thus *ekan* (optionally : *ekāt*) *na viṃśatiḥ* ('not twenty by one' = "19"). VI, 3, 77 states the option of retaining the negative particle unchanged in *naga*, understood to apply to non-moving entities like mountains and trees, while *aga* is used for ambulatory beings when they are stationary.

As to distinguishing the value of the negative particle *na* in a sentence as compared with its value in a negative compound, this is discussed in Iyer's work *Bhartṛhari*.[6] He says that the negation in a compound is expressive *(vācaka)*, while the negation in a sentence is only indicative *(dyotaka)*. The negation in a sentence is never self sufficient, because it always negates something whose non-existence or disappearance is due to other reasons; otherwise stated : an actually existing thing does not disappear merely by use of the negative particle. That is what is meant by saying it is only indicative in a sentence. In contrast, when the negation is in a compound, it acts as an adjective, hence expressing the thing negated. This position holds that while a compound can be made out of a sentence, the meaning of the compound is different, even though maintaining a kind of resemblance with the sentence. In certain types of negative sentences, it is not possible to form a comparable compound; the example Iyer gives is : *brāhmaṇo na bhuṅkte* ('the *brāhmaṇa* does not eat'), and there is no comparable compound, i.e. *abrāhmaṇo (bhuṅkte)*. In the case of the sentence *brāhmaṇo nāsti*, there is the comparable compound *abrāhmaṇaḥ;* however, in the case of the sentence, the negative particle is incapable of denying a *brāhmaṇa*, when translated, "There is no *brāhmaṇa*;" while the compound *abrāhmaṇa* is susceptible of being interpreted in three ways. Of these three ways, if the negative particle is the main term, then *brāhmaṇa* qualifies it, and the compound means : the brahmin's non-existence. If the two terms are in apposition, the second term is the main one, i.e. the compound means : *asan brāhmaṇaḥ* ('the non-existing brahmin'). If the meaning of some other term *(anyapadārtha)* is the main thing, the compound) amounts to : *asad brāhmaṇyam asya* ('one whose brahminhood is non-existent'). This position claims that other negative compounds can also be interpreted in those three ways[7].

Now, this distinction, based on Bhartṛhari's *Vākyapadīya*, of the 'expressive' *(vācaka)* and the merely indicative' *(dyotaka)*, is perhaps exemplified in Nāgārjuna's *Madhyamaka-kārika*, 2nd chap., 1st verse. Here the first *pāda* is *gataṃ na gamyate tāvad*, and the negative particle is presumably 'merely indicative'. Notice that *na . . . tāvat* is susceptible of being compounded as *a-tāvat* ('not equal to them in number') which in association with a verb of motion, *gam-*, would mean 'not so far', and this is 'expressive'. Then the *gamyate* prevalently rendered by previous translators according to its passive form, is susceptible of being interpreted as a reflexive, analogous to *mriyate* and to *dhriyate*.[8] As a relfexive it can be rendered : "does itself go to". So the *pāda* can be translated : "What has finished going to *(gataṃ)* does not itself go to so far." The second *pāda* reads : *āgataṃ naiva gamyate*, which along the same lines can be rendered, "What has not yet gone to *(āgataṃ)* does not itself go to at all." Here, *naiva*, the reinforced negative particle cannot deny the going; the negative compound *āgataṃ* as subject expresses the non-going of what might go.

Gauḍapāda's Kārikā appears to carry on the same kind of talk, in IV, 4 : *bhūtaṃ na jāyate kimcid*. The *na . . . kimcid* can be compounded as *na-kiṃcid* (negative particle remaining unchanged), which means 'nothing'; hence translate the *pāda* : "Nothing that has already been engendered is born." This is followed by, *abhūtaṃ naiva jāyate*, "What has not already been engendered is not born at all." Gaudapāda then states that such sentences support the *Ajāti* (doctrine). According to previous information about Bhartṛhari's position, this expression can be interpreted three ways : (1) the *jāti's* non-existence;

(2) the non-existing *jāti*; (3) one whose *jāti-* nature is non-existent. The sentences appear to illustrate the third interpretation. Note that the third alternative does not state : "One is non-existent by dint of *ajāti*." There is no denial of the carrier, only of his *jāti*. This formulation in *Gauḍapāda-Kārikā* agrees with the *Madhyamaka-kārikā* 2d chap., of pointing to, indicating a situation of potentiality, whether it be a realm of nature or a person, but with no activity or function in evidence. Thus, it is only a vulgar interpretation of either of these two systems that would claim they amount to a denial of the second member of the negative compound, namely, that they are denying *gati* in the one formulation, or denying *jāti* in the other formulation. In this way of talking, it is not possible for *jāti* to become *ajāti* or the reverse; and this is precisely Gauḍapāda's point (IV, 7), "The immortal does not become mortal, nor does the mortal become immortal. For there will never the alternations of (their respective) nature *(prakṛti)*."[9] This is a kind of position where there is a substratum called "the immortal" upon which "the mortal" comes and goes in an illusory manner.

Gauḍapāda's Ajāti doctrine, expressed with the negative particle, was superseded in later Vedānta by the Ātman doctrine, where the mundane superimposition is expressed by the negative compound *anātman*. If one maintains that the term *anātman* is a denial of *ātman*, he has to convert it into a sentence, saying it means "There is no *ātman*," but the negative particle in a sentence is incapable of denying this, as was already mentioned.

Previously it was pointed out that the grammarians claim six senses for the compound with the negative particle as first member. These six interpretations for the negative compound *(nañ-samāsa)* have been studied in a sophisticated manner by Matilal in his "Nañ-vāda" chapter.[10] Here I shall treat them somewhat differently, taking the list and Sanskrit examples from Abhyankar's *A Dictionary of Sanskrit Grammar*.[11] They are (1) *tatsādṛśya* (similarity to it); (2) *tadabhāva* (absence of it); (3) *tadanyatyam* (otherness from it); (4) *tadalpatā* (a small amount of it); (5) *tadaprāśastyam* (detraction of it); (6) *tadvirodha* (opposition to it). The traditional examples for the six senses of the negative are : for similarity to it, *anikṣuḥ śaraḥ* (the *śara* reed is not the sugar-cane reed); for absence of it *bhūtale ghaṭo nāsti* (there is no pot on the spot of ground); for otherness from it, *aghaṭaḥ paṭaḥ* (cloth is not a pot); for a small amount of it, *anudaram udaraṃ taruṇyāḥ* (the girl's belly is a slim belly); for detraction of it, *abrāhmaṇo vārdhuṣikaḥ* (an exactor of high fees is a bad brahmin); for opposition to it, *asuraḥ daityaḥ* (a demon is opposed to the gods).

Those traditional examples barely explain the six senses. For more illustrations, I used the Monier-Williams Sanskrit-English dictionary, the early fascicules of the Poona Sanskrit-English dictionary,[12] and Katre's *Dictionary of Pāṇini*, Part I,[13] as my lexical sources, along with some of my readings in Sanskrit literature. Of course, I am presenting only samples.

1. The set called *tatsādṛśya* (similarity to it) may well have been first in the traditional list for the reason that in the Veda the particle *nā* was used frequently in the sense of 'similar to' and replaced, in this sense, in classical Sanskrit with *iva*. All similarity involves a negation, e.g. a son may resemble his father, who is not him.[14] Matilal gives here the example *a-brāhmaṇaḥ* ('like a brahmin').[15] According to Iyer, this example implies a mistake, later realized; thus, *abrāhmaṇo 'yam kṣattriyaḥ* ('this *kṣattriya* is not a brahmin' — as was supposed; he is only similar to a brahmin).[16] The traditional example *anikṣuḥ* ('not sugar-cane'), suggests a principle of classification, the class of reeds, whose inclusion is the similarity to, while being different from, the sugar-cane reed.

2. The set called *tadabhāva* (absence of it) has such examples as *a-gati* ('absence of access'), *an-aśana* ('abstinence from food'), *an-āgati* ('non-arrival'). There is a host of Bahuvrīhi compounds, such as expressions to be rendered with English suffix-less, e.g. *a-kalaṅka* ('spotless'), *a-pāpa* ('sinless'), *a-prajas* (childless'); or by English 'without', e.g. *an-ādi* ('without a beginning'), *a-kaniṣṭha* ('without a later one or a younger'). When the negative uses of *vi* and *nis-* are added, the adjectival compounds properly to be mentioned here constitute an enormous group of words.

3. The set called *tadanyatva* (otherness from it) is represented by expressions to be rendered by English 'not a . . .' e.g. *a-tad* ('not that'), *an-ātman* ('not self, another'), *a-kāka* (any animal that is not a crow), *a-kāminī*, f. (one who is not a woman'), *a-kṛt* (an affix that is not a *kṛt* affix), *a-gamyā* (woman not to be approached sexually). Besides, there are numerous Bahuvrīhi compounds, typified by *a tajjātiya* ('not of that category'); thus, many gerundives, e.g. *a-nirvacanīya* ('inexpressible'), *an-avadya* ('irreproachable'); many past passive particles, e.g. *an-ukta* ('unsaid'), *an-ārta* ('not sick', 'well'), *a-hīna* ('unimpaired'), *a-gata* (who or which has not gone to, not reached, not moved, not gone forward).

4. The set called *tadalpatā* (a small amount of it) should start with the grammatical example, the *anudarā kanyā* ('very slim girl'). And if understood like translators of Buddhist literature understand the term *an-ātman* (always 'non-soul', and so on), the *anudarā kanyā* to the unwary eye would signify no girl at all, because lacking a belly ! Here is also the *an-ajaka* ('a scrawny goat'), *a-tapas* ('whose austerity leaves much to be desired'). There are also adjectival compounds, such as *abuddhi* (in a commentary, *mandamati* 'dull witted'), *a-catura* (having less than four', 'not cunning or dexterous'), *a-saḍ-akṣa* ('seen by less than six eyes', i.e. a secret known by two persons, by only four eyes).

5. The set called *tadaprāśastyam* (detraction of it) includes *a-dharma* (irreligion), *a-kāla* (wrong time), *a-deśa* (wrong or improper place), *a-pātra* (a worthless vessel), *a-kīrti* (ill-fame, disgrace), *a-kṣaṇa* (unfavourable situations). Among the Bahuvrīhi compounds are *a-rūpa* ('illformed') and *a-karma-kārin* ('performing an evil act').

6. The set called *tadvirodha* (opposition to it) has negative compounds like *avidyā* (nescience), directly opposed to *vidyā* (clear knowledge) in both Hindu and Buddhist commentary; *a-mitra* (this does not mean 'non-friend' but 'enemy', in direct opposition). There are Bahuvīhis like *a-svīkṛta* ('refused', as negation of *svīkṛta* ('assented to'), and *an-uttāna* ('lying face downward' as negation of *uttāna* ('lying face upward'). Also, there is the infinitive *a-kartum* in the meanings 'to undo, to check, control', 'to disobey'.

The negative compounds are not restricted to a single meaning among the six. In illustration, the *a-kartum*, given under the *tadvirodha* class, also has the meaning 'not to do', properly in the *tadanyatvam* class. *Anāmaka* means 'nameless' under *tadabhāva* and 'infamous' under *tadaprāśastyam*. And *a-sa-dṛś*, which under *tadanyatvam* means 'dissimilar', under *tadaprāśastyam* means 'unfit', improper.

Some negative compounds have different meanings while under the same class. Thus *avyaṅga*, under *tadanyatvam*, means 'not mutilated, well-made' but also 'not figurative, plain'. Likewise under *tadanyatvam*, in *Sakuntalā* the king says "*a-sa-varṇa*" ('of a different caste'), but this also means 'not homogenous'.

Another relevant consideration is the comparison of negative compounds with the positive forms. The verbal compound *ni-pat* has many usages according to the dictionaries, starting with 'to fly down' but including a sense 'to fall into (any state)'. Turning to the negative compound *anipadyamāna* ('not falling down to sleep'), 'unretiring', we notice that the negative compound settles on, or limits the meaning to one of the numerous possibilities. It is same with *a-tāvat* ('not equal to them in number'), while the positive form *tāvat* has many usages. Another case is the negative form *an-avara* ('not inferior'), while the positive form *avara* means not only 'inferior' but also 'below', 'younger', 'preceding', and so on. This could be much illustrated, and is presumably a reason for commentators to resort to the negative compound to limit a certain term in a given context. Some examples of this occur in Bhaṭṭōtpala's commentary on Varāhamihira's *Bṛhajjātakam*, chapter on the *nakṣatra*-s.[17] Thus,the person born with moon in *Kṛttikā* is among other descriptions said to be *tejasvin*, having praiseworthy senses, but here an element of blame, and commented *asahiṣṇu* ('not tolerating', i.e. 'hot-tempered'), so I translate "flares up". In the Satabhiṣak case, Bhaṭṭōtpala explains *sāhasika* by *asamīkṣita-vīryavān* so I render it "reckless". For birth in Revatī, the term *saṃpūrṇāṅgaḥ* seems to mean 'having a well filled-in or proportioned body', but is annotated *avikalāvayavah* ('having unimpaired parts'). An infrequent case of Varāhamihira's departure from his prevalent positive terms is when for birth in Mūla he employs the '*dyotaka*' form *nahiṃsraḥ;* and here Bhaṭṭōtpala converts it to the '*vācaka* form *akrurah,* ('without cruel deeds'). Of course, many more examples would have to be collected to justify a general conclusion that the negative compounds specialize the meaning set of a particular positive term, but enough is given here to suggest such a conclusion.

As to whether a study of negative compounds would enable one to understand positive expressions better, this is a hit-and-miss pursuit. Thus, the negative compound *an-ākāśa* ('opaque, not transparent, having no transparent atmosphere') enables us to understand the positive term *ākāśa* to have a possible meaning 'transparent atmosphere'; it also means 'sky'. The term *adravya,* as a noun, 'a nothing, a worthless thing', being in the class *tadaprāśastyam,* does help explain the positive term *dravya* like *adharma* helps explain *dharma,* by providing an extreme case or teaching example.

NOTES AND REFERENCES

1. Srīśa Chandra Vasu, *The Ashtādhyāyī of Paṇini* (reprinted Delhi, 1962) p.290.
2. Vasu, p. 1232.
3. Vasu, p. 258.
4. Vasu, p. 257.
5. Vasu, p. 1233.
6. K. A. Subramania Iyer, *Bhartṛhari* (Poona, 1969), pp. 390 ff.
7. Iyer, p. 392.
8. William Dwight Whitney, *Sanskrit Grammar* (Cambridge, 1941), para. 773, gives only the examples *mriyate* '(himself) dies' and *dhriyate* 'maintains itself; but this is a general possibility for the passive. As to the various translators of *Madhyamaka-kārikā,* Chap. 2, and who, when interpreting *gamyate* as a passive, understood for the line an unexpressed word for road, I need not at this place expatiate upon their difficulties in rendering Nāgārjuna's intention.
9. *nabhavaty amṛtaṃ martyaṃ na martyaṃ amṛtam athā/ prakṛter anyathābhaāvo na kathaṃcid bhaviṣyati/* / (III, 21 = IV, 7).
10. Bimal Krishna Matilal, *The Navya-Nyāya Doctrine of Negation* (Cambridge, 1968), pp. 148-170.
11. K. V. Abhayankar, *A Dictionary of Sanskrit Grammar* (Baroda, 1977), p. 213.
12. *An Encyclopaedic Dictionary of Sanskrit on Historical Principles* (Poona, starting in 1976). The fascicules so far issued of course contain many illustrations of the negative compound with *a-*, but have not advanced to the *an-* compounds in time for the present paper.
13. S. M. Katre, *Dictionary of Pāṇini,* Part I (Poona, 1968).

14. Whitney, *Sanskrit Grammar*, para. 1122h, when giving some examples of the "*nā* of the comparison" says this use is generally explained as being a modification or adaptation of the negative one; "like *(nā)* so-and-so" is equivalent to "not precisely so-and-so".
15. Matilal, *The Navya Nyāya*, p. 148.
16. Iyer, *Bhartṛhari*, p. 394.
17. I use the edition, the Bṛhajjātakam by Varāhamihira, with the Sanskrit Commentary of Bhaṭṭōtpala, edited by Pandit Srī Sītā Rāma Jhā (Benares City, 1934). The *nakṣatra* chapter is no. 16.

3

Sanskrit and Linguistics

LEO PAP

I propose to outline first the status of the Sanskrit language from the viewpoint of general and comparative linguistics, particularly sociolinguistics; that is, from the viewpoints of what the present-day science of linguistics has to say about languages in general, about some specific languages in relation to each other, and about the imbeddedness of a language (such as Sanskrit) in a particular society and culture. I wish next to allude briefly to what the scholarly analysis of the Sanskrit language, in ancient India and in modern times, has contributed to the development of linguistic science.

It was in 1786 that Sir William Jones, a judge in then British India, presented a lecture on the subject of Hindu history and culture before the Asiatic Society of Bengal. Jones had studied Oriental philology at Oxford, then had gone into law, and after his appointment to the bench in Calcutta had become interested in traditional Hindu law, taking up the study of the Sanskrit language in that connection. In his new famous lecture, he said this of Sanskrit : "The Sanskrit language . . . is of a wonderful structure : more perfect than the Greek, more copious than the Latin, and more exquisitely refined than either; yet bearing to both of them a stronger affinity . . . than could have been produced by accident." Sanskrit, Greek and Latin, Jones concluded, must have sprung from a common source — probably together with Gothic (i.e. Germanic), Celtic, and Old Persian; this in view of certain across-the-board similarities in vocabulary and grammar.[1]

Now modern linguists may be divided on whether it is good science to call one language more perfect, wonderful, refined than another. Judgments on perfection are vapid unless hitched to an objective standard; and beauty is in the eyes of the beholder, or in the case of a language, perhaps, in the culturally conditioned ears of a listener. It also depends on who is saying what in what tone of voice. All speech communities have produced poetry along with smut, and judge some speakers more refined or skilled than others. But what William Jones was apparently referring to was the relative transparency or "regularity" of the morphological and morphophonemic structure of Sanskrit, such that a complex word could clearly be broken down into its root, stem, and affixes, and such that variant pronunciations (i.e. forms) of a word, a root, or an ending could be easily reduced to so-called rules of *sandhi* and apophony, as we would say today.

At any rate, Jones' lecture at Calcutta, as printed, stirred up interest in the Sanskrit language among scholars in England, and soon also in France and Germany; prior to that, Europe had been practically ignorant about Sanskrit and the other tongues of India. Of course there had been some contacts between India and the West. As a matter of fact, at the time of Alexander the Great a part of northwestern India was under Greek rule; but the ancient Greeks, just as the ancient Brahmin speakers of Sanskrit themselves, were too ethnocentric to appreciate other languages, which to them were inferior gibberish. It was not until the turn of the 16th century of our era that two Italian travellers, Filippo Sassetti and Roberto de Nobili, noted similarities between a few Sanskrit and Italian words. In the 17th and 18th centuries, a few German, Dutch and French missionaries acquired and spread some knowledge of Sanskrit. But certainly Sir William Jones was the first to posit a genetic relationship between Sanskrit and those several other languages I have mentioned, thereby sparking an interest in what came to be known as comparative and historical linguistics. By 1808 we find the German Friedrich von Schlegel publishing a little book on Sanskrit and Hindu culture. A few years later his brother August Wilhelm von Schlegel became professor of Sanskrit in Bonn, and in 1816 Franz Bopp published a treatise on the verb system of Sanskrit. Linguistics as a science, at first historically oriented, was now born and on its way.[2]

But that is not quite correct, and it is too ethnocentric a statement. To say, as is usually said, that linguistics as an exact empirical science had its start in Europe in the early 19th century is probably justified if we compare the precision and breadth of modern linguistic scholarship with the most speculative and unsystematic ponderings on the subject of language that had gone on before in most of the world, for three thousand years or longer. But there is one glaring exception, viz., the descriptive analysis of the Sanskrit language performed by some ancient Indian grammarians. It is on account of this that India, in the words of Professor Emeneau, may be considered the cradle of linguistics. Or, as Professor Robins put it, linguistics in India goes back further than in Europe, and it was more advanced than anything achieved in Europe before contact had been made with Indian linguistic work.[3] Leonard Bloomfield, the leading American linguist some 50 years ago, paid homage to Pāṇini's grammar of Sanskrit, probably composed during the 6th to 5th century before Christ, as "one of the greatest monuments of human intelligence"; "no other language, to this day, has been so perfectly described", in Bloomfield's opinion.[4] More on this a little later.

What exactly is the status of Sanskrit in relation to other languages, according to present-day linguistic scholarship ? In its preclassical stage at least, Sanskrit can be called the oldest language within the language family referred to as Indo-European of which we have any detailed documented knowledge. I am not suggesting that it is the oldest language in the world; we shall probably never know when and where human speech originated. Nor is it implied that there were ever any people who called their own language "Indo-European". This is the label given to a hypothetical language reconstructed by modern linguists precisely to explain the apparent similarities between Sanskrit, Greek, Latin and many other languages of past and present. Moreover, all natural human languages, as far as we know, are subject to change, although, after a certain amount of change has occurred, a given language may be given a new name and thus be considered a different language. In rare cases only and this is the case of Sanskrit, a language may be artificially codified and rigidified so as to undergo little or no change thereafter — but typically at the expense of losing its function as an overall medium of everyday communication.

Speakers of a particular offshoot of Indo-European, of a particular dialect or bundle of closely related dialects — Indo-Iranian or Aryan — had moved across Iran into northwestern India, to conquer and mingle with "indigenous" people there speaking early forms of what we now call the Dravidian, Munda and perhaps other languages. These dominant Indo-Aryans, speakers of what linguists now label Old Indic, considered their own language as divine, as the only true and natural reflection of thought and reality, capable of magic powers. The older non-Aryan population elements, the "Amerindians of India", were looked down upon as subhuman.[5] Early and later forms of Old Indic are preserved for us in the approximately 1,000 hymns of the Vedas, metric religious poems composed between perhaps 1,500 and 800 B.C. The Vedic hymns embodying the old Brahmin religion were transmitted only orally until the invention of the Devanagari script. Because of the belief in word magic that usually inheres in religious rituals, it was very important to the ancient Hindus to preserve the exact original text and pronunciation of the Vedas, in the face of the natural changes and dialectal divergences affecting Old Indic speech over the generations, as regards phonology, grammar, and vocabulary. Sanskrit in the narrower sense, known as Classical Sanskrit (as against the older Vedic), resulted from the attempt to stem the tide of change through standardization.[6]

To be exact, the language generally referred to as Sanskrit was not a direct descendant of Vedic, but of a spoken dialect close to it. Whether classical Sanskrit was ever the colloquial *everyday* idiom of any group of Hindus is not entirely clear. At most it was the educated, relatively formal, speech of the priestly upper caste of Brahmins, centered in the Punjab at first and later spreading to eastern parts of the country. Other dialects of Indo-Aryan or Old Indic, not directly documented, spoken by the lower castes and increasingly also by Brahmins, led to the Middle Indic vernaculars, or "Prakrits", such as Pali, covering the period from about 400 B.C. to 1,000 A.D. Through the influence of the Brahmins and because of the growing divergence of regional Indian idioms, classical Sanskrit was adopted as a second language, or "lingua franca", by other ethnic groups within India, for learned discourse, governmental communication, and literature. Sanskrit thus acquired a status comparable to that of Latin in Europe's Middle Ages. A rough parallel can also be drawn between the Prakrits of Middle Indic and the early Romance idioms (Old Spanish, Old French, Old Portuguese, etc.), which derived largely from variants of Vulgar Latin rather than directly from classical literary Latin. (Incidentally, the modern Indian languages of Indo-European descent, i.e. exclusive of Dravidian and so forth, did not derive directly from the standard Middle Indic Prakrits either, but rather from the so-called Apabhraṃśas, strictly colloquial speech forms current in India about the same time as Old Romance and Old English in western Europe.)[7]

Even though the Brahmins as guardians of the Vedic hymns (and of the associated socio-religious system) tried to preserve the sacred texts against any change, they could not prevent gradual changes in their own day-by-day upper-class speech, and much less so in the speech of the common people. In the post-Vedic period, say by the 7th or 6th century B.C., the language of the early Vedic texts began to look markedly archaic, requiring some commentary. This led to a self-conscious interest in language analysis, and thus to the development of phonetics, etymology, and grammar. Little is known about the earliest scholarly work of this kind; it is overshadowed by the Sanskrit grammar of Pāṇini, compiled about the 5th or the 4th century B.C. as I have already indicated.

Pāṇini's description of Sanskrit presumably represents his own careful upper-class speech, and it is very close to the language of the so-called Sūtras (instructions for performing various rituals), composed centuries after Vedas. This classical Sanskrit differs from the poetic Vedic language, and to a lesser extent from the prose of the Brahmanas (interpretations of rituals), in features such as these : The earlier pitch or tone accent is becoming more of a stress accent (as happened in the history of Latin); the semantic distinction between the three past tenses of Vedic (comparable to the Imperfect, Aorist, and Perfect of Ancient Greek) is largely lost and so is the subjunctive; there is a marked preference for passive rather than active verb phrases — resulting overall in simplified inflexion. Compound nouns, usually confined to two components in Vedic, may now consist of half a dozen or more simple nouns, as is true for English and German in our day. In vocabulary, there is an increasing infiltration of Prakrit and also of non Indo-European (mostly Dravidian) words.[8]

Pāṇini's Sanskrit Grammar — which incorporates observations by many unnamed predecessors — is characterized by extraordinary conciseness. It has been praised (for instance by Bloomfield) as the most complete description of any language; I would specify, though, that this reputed comprehensiveness is in phonetics/phonology and morphology, more than in syntax, semantics, or lexicon. The grammar consists of about 4,000 aphoristic rules in a set order, using various abbreviations or algebraic notations convenient for oral memorizing — but incomprehensible without commentary. Such commentaries were later supplied by Patañjali and other Indian linguists. In his succinct formalism, Pāṇini somewhat anticipated the formalistic rule-ordered presentations of current transformational-generative grammar. Modern developments in linguistics are also foreshadowned by Pāṇini's distinction between surface and underlying "cases" (think of case grammar !) in relating nouns to verbs, and the use of connotation-free numerals rather than of semantic labels (such as nominative, genitive) to distinguish the cases of Sanskrit. Also Pāṇini introduced the "zero" notion for forms where a grammatical category has no overt representation (as in the English word *sheep*, where we say the plural is marked by "zero", etc.).[9]

As I have already hinted, Pāṇini's grammar was only one, although the most impressive work of ancient Indian linguistics, inspired by the Brahmin desire to fix the language of old sacred texts, in the form which, in contradistinction to the naturally evolving vernaculars, the Prakrits, came to be known as Sanskrit (literally meaning something like "artfully fashioned", "perfected") Mostly after Pāṇini's time, and apart from commentaries dealing directly with his formulas, we encounter rather advanced treatises in articulatory phonetics, beginnings in lexicography, and general grammatical theory, including the distinction between *sphoṭa* and *dhvani* which in a way anticipated the modern distinction between "emic" and "etic", "langue" and "parole".[10] In the Western world, where Sanskrit became well known by the early part of the 19th century, serious research on ancient Indian linguistics began in the 1880's; there has been an intensified interest in it among followers of Chomskyan TG grammar since the mid-1960's.[11]

What about the current status of Sanskrit, not in the scholarly world of linguistics and of Indology but in the practical affairs of multilingual modern India ? Sanskrit had lost its position as the official state language of India when Persian took over, about 1,000 years ago, but it continued as a prestigious medium of learned and literary intercourse, somewhat longer than Latin in Europe. All along there was also a heavy infusion of Sanskrit vocabulary into other Indian languages. After the British had conquered India, English naturally made inroads, as against Sanskrit and Persian, as a language of government and as a lingua franca of cultured discourse. For lexican borrowings, into various modern vernaculars, adherents of Hindu religion veered toward Sanskrit, Muslims toward Persian.

After the partition of India, Urdu, the stylistic variety of the modern Hindustani idiom leaning toward Persian and Arabic became the official language of Pakistan, whereas Hindi, the Sanskrit-oriented variety, became the official language of present-day India — a country which, at the level of everyday spoken communication, is still extraordinarily multilingual : About 70% of the toal population are native speakers of some 17 different languages of Indo-European descent; some 15%, centered in South India, speak at least four different languages of Dravidian stock; and there are scores of other minor tongues. Sanskrit is said to be still the major source of lexical borrowings and of new coinages.[12]

The pervasive influence of Sanskrit as the vehicle of much traditional Indian "high culture" is reflected by the fact that the term "Sanskritization" is now sometimes used to refer to culture rather than to language, namely, to the process by which a lower caste attempts to raise its status through the adoption of rituals, customs, and beliefs associated with high-status groups.[13] Sanskrit as a literary language has thus remained a symbol of prestige and refinement in much of Indian society.

NOTES AND REFERENCES

1. Winfred P. Lehmann, ed. : *A Reader in Nineteenth-Century Historical Indo-European Linguistics* (Bloomington : Indiana Univ. Press, 1967). pp. 7, 10, 15, Louis H. Gray : *Foundations of Language* (New York : Macmillan, 1939), pp. 434-37.
2. Gray, *loc. cit.* Holger Pedersen : *The Discovery of Language* (Bloomington : Indiana Univ. Press 1962), pp. 17-20.`
3. Murray B. Emeneau : "India and Linguistics", 1955; cf. *language,* v. 58, no. 1 (March 1982), p. 186. R. H. Robins : *A Short History of Linguistics* (London: Longmans Green, 1965), p. 136.
4. Leonard Bloomfield : *Language* (New York : Hot, 1933), p. 11.
5. Arno Borst : *Der Turmbau von Babel,* v. 1 (Stuttgart : Hiersmann, 1957), pp. 58-61. Madhav M Deshpande : *Sociolinguistic Attitudes in India* (An Arbor : Karoma 1979), pp. 1-2.
6. Cf. Robins, *op. cit.*, p. 136. Pedersen, *op. cit.*, pp. 14-15. Vilhelm Thomsen: *Geschichte der Sprachwissenschaft* . . . (Halle : Max Niemeyer, 1927), p. 3.
7. Gray, *op. cit.*, pp. 314-16. Winifred P. Lehmann : *Historical Linguistics,* 2nd ed. (New York : Hot, 1973), pp. 22-23. Ram Gopal : *Linguistic Affairs of India* (Bombay : Asia Publishing House, 1966), pp. 1-4. T. Burrow : *The Sanskrit Language* (London : Faber & Faber, 1955), pp. 2, 44-55, 57-60.
8. Burrow, *op. cit.*, pp. 35-44, 53-57. Deshpande, *op. cit.*, pp. 3-4.
9. Robins, *op. cit.*, pp. 137, 144-48. Winfred P. Lehmann (review of Deshpande: "Evolution of Syntactic Theory in Sanskrit Grammar," *Word,* v. 32, no. 3 (December 1981), pp. 245-249. Thomsen, *op. cit.*, p. 7. Hans Arens : *Sprachwissenschaft* (Freiburg : Alber, 1955), pp. 146-47. Winfred P. Lehmann : *Language, an Introduction* (New York : Random House, 1983), p.2. Burrow, *op. cit.*, pp. 49-51.
10. Robins, *op. cit.*, pp. 137-143 Burrow, *op. cit.*, 47-51.
11. Cf. Rosanne Rocher : "Studies in the Indian Grammarians", *Semiotica,* v. 12 (1974), pp. 263-80. On the direct impact of the old Sanskrit grammarians upon modern linguistics, see also Bloomfield, *op. cit.*, p. 208; Pedersen, *op. cit.*, pp. 22-23; Francis P. Dinneen : *Introduction to General Linguistics* (New York : Holt, 1967), p. 311.
12. Ram Gopal, *op. cit.*, pp. 1, 4-5, 16-18, 46, 252-253. Deshpande, *op. cit.*, p. 65. Burrow, *op. cit.*, pp.62-63.
13. J. F. Staal : "Sanskrit and Sanskritization", *Journal of Asian Studies,* v. 22, no. 3 (1963), pp. 261-75.

4

Semantics of Kārakas in Pāṇini : An Exploration of Philosophical and Linguistic Issues

MADHAV M. DESHPANDE

The system of *kārakas* is an important landmark in the history of syntactic theories. In recent decades, more attention has been paid to this aspect of Pāṇinian grammar by Sanskritists and linguists than to any other. Important controversies have occupied the attention of such scholars as George Cardona, S. D. Joshi, Paul Kiparsky and others, and through this stimulating debate our understanding of Pāṇini system is gradually inching forward. The most difficult problem of the current Pāṇinian research is how to use the help provided by the traditional commentators and modern developments in linguistics, without at the same time being influenced by these ancient and modern guides to a degree where we would begin imposing anachronistic views on Pāṇini. While it must be openly admitted that each generation of Pāṇinian scholars has its share in developing its own anachronistic conceptions of Pāṇini and while it is also true that we cannot do without the aid offered by our predecessors in this field, we must, nevertheless, watch every step and make sure that we do not accept an image of Pāṇini in a particular mirror without attempting to find out the original source of the image.

In terms of syntactic considerations, the recent research seems to have conclusively established at least two points: directionality of Pāṇini's grammar and the existence of various successive stages or levels in the process of derivation. To the tradition of Sanskrit commentators, it was never totally clear whether Pāṇini's grammar had this sense of directionality, i.e. whether it proceeded from meaning to form or vice versa. For a grammarian like Patañjali the statements *tum-artho bhāvaḥ* "the meaning of *-tum* is action", and *bhāve tum* "*-tum* occurs (or is used) to denote action" are virtually equivalent statements. Commentatorial discussions can and do proceed in both directions.[1] This is partly inevitable because the tradition uses Pāṇini's grammar as a means for interpreting Vedic and classical texts, a process which must indeed proceed from the words of a given text to its meaning being established. However, modern scholars have now determined that Pāṇini's grammar is a device to encode a given meaning and produce an expression, and not to interpret or decode a given expression and find out its meaning. The work of Van Nooten (1969) and Bronkhorst (1979) must be particularly mentioned in this context, though many other scholars have also touched upon this subject. This determination is not really surprising. This runs parallel to the nature of the *Prātiśākhya* texts. These texts already assume the existence of the analytical *Padapāṭha* ("Word-by-word text") of the Vedas and then give rules to build (actually to *re*-build) the *Saṁhitāpāṭha* ("continuous text"). They do not tell us how to break down the *Saṁhitāpāṭha* into the *Padapāṭha*. Similarly, contrary to the belief of the nineteenth century Sanskrit scholarship, Pāṇini's grammar does not provide us with analytical tools to go from texts to their interpretation, or from sentences to morphemes and phonemes. It presupposes the results of an analytical phase of scholarship, but is itself not representative of that analytical phase. It goes from meaning to form; from morphemes to sentences. This understanding may seem to be a trivial advance, but one needs only to remember the earlier views of Pāṇini's system which totally underestimated the role of syntax and semantics.

The second accomplishment of the recent research is to have discovered that Pāṇinian grammar and its derivational processes move along a certain progression of steps and stages from meaning to form. This progression is a continuum. For instance, Kiparsky and Staal (1969:84) point out : "Pāṇini's grammar is a system of rules for converting semantic representations of sentences into phonetic representations via two intermediate levels which may be respectively compared with the level of deep (underlying) structure and surface structure in a generative grammar". Though Cardona differs from

Kiparsky and Staal on many points, he still affirms this general direction of progression. Speaking about Pāṇini's *kāraka* categories, Cardona (1976:220) says: "This *(kāraka)* categorization serves an intermediary between semantics and grammatical expressions derived by rules of the grammar." Kiparsky in his recent work (1982:26ff) again returns to this theme of progression of levels in Pāṇini and offers a slightly revised formulation of how these levels are related to each other in Pāṇini's grammar. However, despite the differences in the earlier and the later revised ideas, the notion of progression of levels is still maintained. This notion of successive levels combined with the concept that Pāṇini's grammar is a grammar of encoding meaning advances our understanding of his system significantly, and allows us to pose further questions to be investigated. But, first a brief outline of the *kāraka* system.

Briefly stated, a *kāraka* is something that helps to bring about an action *(kriyājanaka)*. This is a broad concept. For instance, in a sentence such as: *rāmaḥ vahninā sthālyām odanam pacatti* "Rama cooks rice in a pot by means of fire", the agent *(kartr)*: Rama, the object *(karman)*; rice, the locus *(adhikaraṇa)*; pot and the instrument or means *(karaṇa)*; fire are factors such that all of them contribute in their own ways to bring about the action of cooking, and are thus to be called *kārakas*, in a preliminary sense.

Each *Kāraka* definition contains two important elements. The general structure may be given in the following manner:" If an entity *E* fulfils a certain role *x* with respect to a given action, then that entity *E* is given the grammatical designation *y* with respect to that particular action". There are six such *kāraka* designations, but each of them subsumes many different roles. Thus, there are many more rules than designations.[2] Words convey certain meanings, and these meanings reflect a language-specific pattern of perceiving and classifying the world.[3] Given these word-meanings which are semantic segments of a world-conception, Pāṇini proposes a further classification of these semantic segments in terms of their roles with respect to a given action signified by a given verb. Particular semantic segments fulfilling particular roles are given certain grammatical designations. These are the *kāraka* designations. These designations are then used to predict particular case-endings for the particular nominals in question. For a general understanding, see Diagram [A] Major *kāraka* designations and some important rules which operate the system of predicting case-endings are given below.

MAJOR *KĀRAKA* RULES

P.1.4.1 *(ā kaḍārād ekā samjnā)*: "Up to the word *Kaḍāra*, only designation (applies at a time)".

P.1.4.2 *(vipratiṣedhe param kāryam)*: "In a case of conflict, the latter of two conflicting rules prevails (in this section)".

P.1.4.23 *(Kārake)*: "Among items which help bring about an action". (This is a heading which continues into the following rules.)

P.1.4.24 *(dhruvam apāye' pādānam)*: "That which is the (relatively firm point when departure takes place is given the designation *apādāna*."

P.1.4.32 *(karmanā yam abhipraiti sa sampradānam)* : "That for which (the agent) intends the object of his action is given the designation *sampradāna*."

P.1.4.42 *(sādhakatamam karaṇam)*: "The means par excellence is given the designation *karaṇa*.

P.1.4.43 *(divaḥ karma ca)*: "The means par excellence in the case of the verb *div* 'to play dice' is also given the designation *karma*."

P.1.4.45 *(ādhāro dhikaraṇam)*: "That which is the locus is given the designation *adhikaraṇa*."

P.1.4.46 *(adhi-śīṅ-sthāsāṁ karma)*: "The locus, in the case of the verbs' *ī*, *sthā* and *ās* with the prefix *adhi*, is given the designation *karma*."

P.1.4.49 *(kartṛur īpsitatamaṁ karma)*: "That which the agent most seeks to encompass (with his action, or simply accomplish) is given the designation *karma*."

A SAMPLE OF CASE-PREDICTION RULES

P.2.3.1 *(anabhihite)*: "If not (already) expressed (by some other element)." (This continues into the following rules.)

P.2.3.2 *(karmaṇi dvitīyā)*: "The second triplet of case-endings is added to a nominal to express the object, if the notion of objecthood has not already expressed otherwise."

PANINI'S *KARAKA* SYSTEM

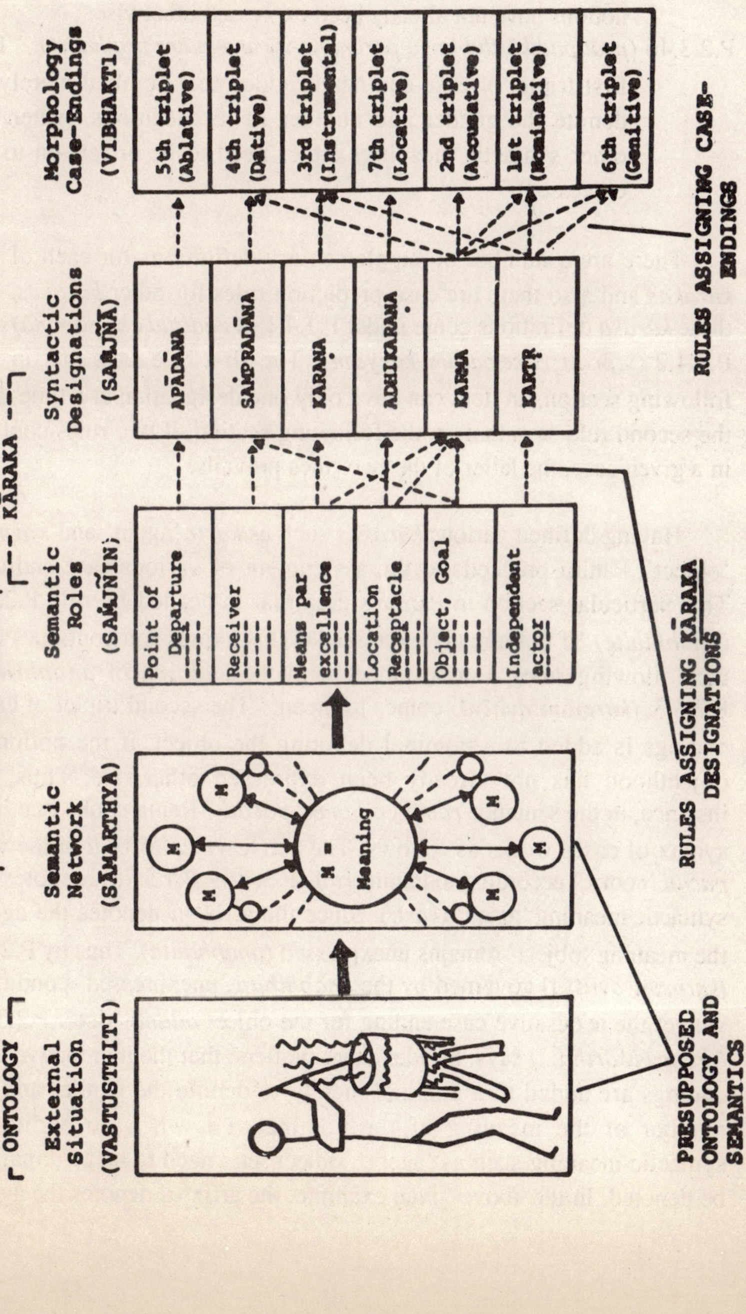

P.2.3.18 *(kartṛkaraṇayas tṛtīyā)*: "The third triplet of case-endings is added to a nominal to denote the agent or instrument, if these notions have not already been expressed otherwise.

P.2.3.46 *(prātipadikārtha-linga-parimāṇa-vacana-mātre prathamā)*: "The first triplet of case-endings is added to a nominal merely to denote the gender and number of its meanings, (when no other syntactic meanings either need to be or remain to be expressed)."

There are a number of supplementary definitions for each of the *kārakas* and also there are case-prediction rules for other *kārakas*. All these *kāraka* definitions come under P.1.4.1 (*ā kaḍārād ekā samjnā*) and P.1.4.2 *(vipratiṣedhe paraṁ kāryam)*. The first rule says that in the following section, an item can have only one designation at a time, and the second rule says that, in the following section, if two rules conflict in a given case, the latter of the two rules prevails.

Having defined various *kārakas* such as *kartṛ* 'agent' and *karman* 'object', Pāṇini proceeds to the assignment of various case-endings. This particular section in Pāṇini's grammar is headed by rule P.2.3.1 *(anabhihite)* 'if not already expressed'. This expression continues into the following rules. For instance, with the addition of *anabhihite*, P.2.3.3. *(karmaṇi dvitīyā)* comes to mean: "The second triplet of case-endings is added to a nominal denoting the object, if the notion of objecthood has not already been expressed otherwise."Thus, for instance, in the sentence *rāmaḥ odanam pacati* 'Rama cooks rice,' the syntax of cases works as follows. The active voice affix-*ti* in the verb *pacati* 'cooks,' according to Pāṇini (ref. P.3.4.69 P.1.3.78), denotes the syntactic meaning 'agent' (*kartṛ*). Since the affix -*ti* denotes the agent, the meaning 'object' remains unexpressed (*anabhihita*). Thus by P.2.3.2 *(karmaṇi dvitīyā)* governed by the *anabhihita* 'unexpressed' condition, we get the accusative case ending for the object *odana* 'rice'. P.2.3.46 *(pratipadikārtha...)* says, besides other matters, that the nominative case endings are added to a nominal merely to denote the gender and the number of the meaning of the nominal, i.e. when no additional syntactic meaning such as 'agent','object' etc. need to be or remain to be denoted. In the above-given example, the affix -*ti* denotes the agent, and hence this particular syntactic meaning does not need to be or remain to be denoted. Therefore, by P.2.3.46, we get the residual nominative case for the agent *rāma*. This briefly explains the "expressed/ unexpressed" control mechanism in Pāṇini's grammar. The above discussion also brings out an important point concerning the centrality of a verb in Pāṇinian syntax. The choice of affixes which go on the verb is obviously made prior to the choice of affixes which go on the related nominals. One starts with a verb and then predicts cases in related nouns, rather than starting with nouns and then proceeding to the verb. This is another directional factor.

In dealing with the *kārakas*, we are primarily dealing with a linguistic world-view of the world which is to some extent colored and restricted, as well as facilitated, by the screen of a given language. We are not dealing with the world "as it is", but with the world as it is *conventionally* perceived by a given community. Thus the "roles" in these *kāraka* rules are not necessarily a part of the real world as it is out there, but a part of a culture-specific and a language-specific interpretation of the world as it is perceived by an individual. In simple terms, it depends upon the intention of the speaker *(vivakṣātaḥ kārakāṇi bhavanti)* in a conventionalized form. There is freedom within the limits of cultural and linguistic conventions. The *kāraka* designations represent a further step than the classifications of the perceived world into "roles". These designations readjust these roles to suit the purposes of grammar. If a number of roles are represented by a single grammatical item, than all of these different roles may be given a single *kāraka* designation. However, if the same role is represented by more than one grammatical item alternatively, then one and the same role could be given more than one designation. The motives behind this reclassification are mainly linguistic or grammatical, and not logical or ideational. There is no necessary one-to-one correspondence between the roles and designations, or even between the designations and the case-terminations. From the semantic world to case-terminations, there are a number of adjustments, and these adjustments are reflected in the formulation of *kāraka* rules and the rules of case-prediction.

For instance, P.1.4.43 *(divaḥ karma ca, sādhakatamaṁ karaṇam* from 42) says that the means par excellence in the case of the verb *div* "to play dice" is also given the designation *karman* ("object"), in addition to the normal designation *karaṇa* ("instrument"). Thus a semantic segment fulfilling the role of "means par excellence", in the case of a particular verb, is optionally reclassified either as an "Instrument" or "Object". This optional reclassification of the same role in a specific context is important in the face of the fact that the assignment of case-endings to nominal stems is defined by Pāṇini directly in terms of these designations, and not directly in terms of the semantic roles. For instance, Pāṇini's assignment of the second triplet of case-endings by rule P.2.3.2 *(karmaṇi dvitīyā)* rests completely on the assignment of the grammatical designation *karman*, and not upon any particular semantic role. In some cases, the accusative ending may signify "something which the agent most seeks to encompass with his action", while in the case of the verb *div*, the same case-ending signifies the role "means par excellence". Here in both cases the accusative case ending refers to items which have the same *kāraka* designation, i.e. *karman*. But, in one case the designation applies to "something which the agent most seeks to encompass with his action", while in another case it applies to an "instrument". Thus, in terms of what the accusative ending means to express, one must point not to the *kāraka* designation, but to the semantic role. This is a very significant distinction, which has not always been observed by the traditional commentators on *Pāṇini*. To queries concerning the meanings of case-endings, the traditional commentators frequently reply by referring to the *kāraka* designations.[4] This is not quite appropriate. The *kāraka* designations are purely technical devices to interface semantic roles and the morphological categories. In themselves, these designations are not semantic categories.

There is a considerable amount of ontological speculation concerning the concept of *kāraka* in the works of Sanskrit grammarians. Patanjali discusses the question of whether *kāraka* refers to a substance in its entirely, or to just a property thereof. He presents two alternative views on this subject. As part of this discussion, Patanjali says:[5]

> Is it the substance (as a whole) which is the means (of bringing about an action), or is it rather just a property (of a substance which is the means of bringing about an action)?...We say that it is a property (of a substance which is the means of bringing about an action). How is this known? (The argument is as follows).
>
> Someone asks a person: "Where is Devadatta?"
> That person tells him: He is on a tree."
> "On which tree?"
> "(On that tree) which stands here."
>
> That tree first becomes a locus, and later, when expressed by another word, it becomes an agent. If the means of bringing about an action were the substance as a whole, then whatever is an object *(karman)* in one context will always be an object, and whatever is a locus *(adhikaraṇa)* (in one context will always be) a locus.

This implies that, for Patañjali, a substance has various properties, and each property may work independently to bring about some action in some peculiar way. For this reason, the same tree can become a locus in the sentence "He is on that tree", and can later become the agent of the sentence "That tree stands here". There is an important message here for us. The *kāraka* roles are not to be determined purely by looking at the "silent movie" of a given situation, but are to be determined by taking into account the factor of intentionality *(vivakṣā)*.[6] For all practical purposes, we may assume that there is a world out there. Then, there is a conception of the world or of a given situation that a person has. This conception of the world is not produced by the person by being a neutral receiver. He is a maker of this conception, and his intentionality plays a great role in the resulting shape of this conception. This intended conception of a situation may be described by using Pāṇini's semantic terminology, i.e. categories such as *svatantra* "independent", *sādhakatama* "means par excellence", *ādhāra* "locus" etc. Pāṇini uses this semantic terminology to formulate his rules assigning particular syntactic designations. At this juncture, there are numerous questions, some of which have received attention. However, there is obviously more room for further investigation. In what follows, I will explore the question of whether there is only one level of meaning or whether there are multiple levels, and also the role of the notion of intentionality *(vivakṣā)* in the operation of Pāṇini's *kāraka* system.

One may make a distinction between an ontological level of the world as it is and a level of linguistic intentionality which presents a particular configuration of that world in terms of how the speaker intends to talk about it. This distinction is not new. Cardona (1974:238) says: "In this connection, it is worthwhile reemphasizing a point made before [Cardona 1967, Kiparsky-Staal 1969:109], namely that Pāṇini's *kāraka* classifications are not principally ontological. Pāṇiniyas stress that the *kāraka* rules class things not as they are but as they are spoken of." I fully agree with this view of Cardona. However, citing extensive passages from Patañjali, Cardona further concludes that one cannot simply let the speaker's intention *(vivakṣā)* carry the burden. In his opinion, there must be a mechanism which controls the speaker's intention, and that mechanism is Pāṇini's rules: P.1.4.1 *(ā kaḍarād ekā saṁjnā)* and P.1.4.2 *(vivpratisedhe paraṁ kāryam)*. The first rules says, as we have seen before, that in the following section only one designation applies at a time, and the second rules says that in a case where there is a possibility of two designations applying simultaneously, the latter designation prevails. Cardona takes this as a principal which in part is intended to control the speaker's intention. S.D. Joshi and J.A.F. Roodbergen are also of the same view. Joshi-Roodbergen (1975:xviff) argue for this view and criticize Candragomin's grammar for a supposed lack of similar devices.[7] It is clear that these scholars base their opinion on certain discussions in Patañjali's *Māhabhāṣya*. We shall briefly review this argument below.

On P.1.4.1, Kātyāyana and Patañjali discuss the purposes if this rule and the one following this. Kātyāyana argues[8] that one needs this procedure so that in case of conflict, the later *kārakas* may supersede the *apādāna kāraka*. To illustrate this point, Kātyāyana considers the following examples:

[A] **dhanuṣaḥ vidhyati* "X shoots (an arrow) with a bow".
[B] *dhanuṣā vidhyati* "X shoots (an arrow) with a bow".

The argument is as follows. When someone shoots *(vidhyati)* an arrow by using a bow, the bow is at the same time a point of departure for the arrow as well as a means to accomplish the action of shooting. The first characterization as a point of departure would earn for it the *kāraka* designation *apādāna* by P.1.4.24 *(dhruvam apāye' pādānam),* while the second characterization would earn for it the designation *karaṇa* by P.1.4.42 *(sādhakatamaṁ karaṇam).* Then P.1.4.1 and P.1.4.2 come in and say that of these two simultaneously applicable designations, the latter prevails, and therefore we get only *dhanuṣā vidhyati,* and can prevent the derivation of **dhanuṣaḥ vidhyati".* Similarly, in the same context, Kātyāyana considers the following pair:

[A] **dhanuṣaḥ vidhyati* "X shoots (an arrow) from a bow".
[C] *dhanuḥ vidhyati* "The bow shoots (an arrow)".

The argument here is similar. When someone shoots by using a bow, the bow as a point of departure for the arrow gets the designation *apādāna* by P1.4.24. However, the same bow, if one looks only at its own contribution to the act of shooting and does not think of the main agent, may be viewed as being "independent" *(svatantra),* and then be given the designation *kartṛ* "agent" by P.1.4.54 *(svatantraḥ kartā).* Again, in this apparent conflict, P.1.4.1 and P.1.4.2 dictate that the latter term will prevail and one would get only the nominative usage *dhanuḥ vidhyati*, as Kātyāyana supposedly desired. This is the discussion in Patañjali's *Mahabhāṣya* which has influenced the opinion of scholars such as Cardona, Joshi and Roodbergen.

What is this discussion supposed to mean for our understanding of Pāṇini's syntax? One may consider various possible alternatives. Is it that when there are multiple ontological possibilities for a given item, the rules P.1.4.1-2 come in and help retain one of those ontological possibilities? Or is it the case that when a person has several intentions simultaneously, these rules control his intentions? Do these rules control ontological possibilities, or do they control multiple intentionalities? Is it the claim that Pāṇini's grammar dictates a person's intentionality? These are the kinds of possibilities one must consider in dealing with this area of Pāṇinian syntax. While Cardona, Joshi and Roodbergen have done their best to fathom the secrets of these issues, we will explore them further to see if we can arrive at some different conclusions. This reinvestigation becomes all the more necessary because the ancient commentators do not present to us a single consolidated position, as it may appear from previous studies, but they present to us an array of various possible alternatives. In what follows, I shall attempt to sort out these different views found in the *Māhabhāṣya,* and to see if any of them appears to be more convincing than others.

The views discussed by Kātyāyana and Patañjali concerning the significance of P.1.4.1-2 may be sorted out largely into three views, with I shall label as views[A], [B] and [C].

VIEW [A] : RULE-ORDERING CONTROLS SIMULTANEOUS MULTIPLE ROLES

This is essentially the same as the view discussed earlier, and has appeared in Cardona (1974) and Joshi-Roodbergen (1975 : xviff). This is based on Kātyāyana's *vārttikas* and Patañjali's *Mahābhāṣya* on P.1.4.1. The standard arguments and examples for this view have been given earlier. To recapitulate, one cannot think of a bow as the agent of the action of shooting an arrow, without also thinking of it as the point of departure. Given these multiple simultaneous categorizations, P.1.4.1.-2 tell us that the designation *kartṛ* "agent" prevails over the designation *apādāna.*

While the texts clearly argue for the eixstence of multiple simultaneous classifications for a given item, they really do not clarify a further dimension. The texts do not say clearly if these multiple simultaneous classifications are purely simultaneous ontological or logical possibilities, which exist irrespective of one's intentionality, or whether in this particular case, for these ontological or logical possibilities to come under the jurisdiction of P.1.4.1-2, they must also be simultaneous intentions. The characterization of this position by Cardona, Joshi and Roodbergen would have us think that there would have to be simultaneous multiple intentionality to create a conflict under P.1.4.1, which would then be resolved by P.1.4.2. But this notion of multiple simultaneous intentionality is not clearly reflected in the texts themselves.

VIEW [B] : RULE-ORDERING CREATES PROBLEMS WITH A VIEW : "ALL *KĀRAKAS* ARE POTENTIAL *KARTṚS*"

This view is basically a kind of *pūrva-pakṣa* "prima facie" view brought up by Kātyāyana and Patañjali *(Varttika* 14 on P.1.4.23, *Mahābhāṣya*, Vol. I, p. 325). This view is based on an analysis of the *kārakas* which attempts to show that in fact each *kāraka* contributes its own action as part of the main action. The main action is nothing more than a grouping of the actions of all relevant *kārakas*. Thus, when one says that "Devadatta cooks rice in a pot", the action of cooking is essentially a cover-term which includes actions being carried out by all the contributing *kārakas*. Thus, the pot does the act of containing and holding the rice, and is in fact the agent *(kartṛ)* of this subordinate action. Thus, idealy, each *kāraka* is a *kartṛ* "agent" of a subordinate action which it contributes to the main action.[9] Thus, a *kāraka* such as the pot above is dependent *(paratantra)* as an instrument on the action of the main agent, but is independent *(svatantra)* with respect to its own action of holding and containing rice etc., and hence is the agent of that action. Thus, each *kāraka* has these simultaneous dependent and independent roles and hence simultaneous multiple classifications.

Given such a situation, the objector[10] says that the designation *kartṛ* "agent" which comes after all the other *kāraka* designations will prevail over all of them by the rule-ordering principles given by P.1.4.1-2, and hence we will not be able to actually have any other designation except *kartṛ* "agent". In a given sentence, all factors contributing to bring about an action would then appear as *kartṛs*.

Even in describing this objection, Patañjali does not bring in the notion of *vivakṣā* "speaker's intention". He says that since there is *(vidyate)* simultaneous dependence *(pāratantrya)* and independence *(svātantrya)* for each *kāraka*, the above dilemma would occur because of rule-ordering. He does not bring up the notion of intention either to state his problem or to state the basic conception of each *kāraka* being a potential *kartṛ* "agent". Thus, the underlying conceptions here are ontological or logical, but they do not involve the notion of intentionality.

The objection raised here by Kātyāyana and Patañjali is a very interesting objection to the notion of rule-ordering. While these ancient grammarians do not use this objection directly against View[A] described earlier, it could very well apply to it. If rule-ordering is valid as well as the underlying conception of each *kāraka* being a potential *kartṛ* "agent", then of the examples A, B and C discussed earlier, one could finally derive only C, and not be able to derive either A or B.

A.	* *dhanuṣaḥ vidhyati*	*(apādāna)*
B.	*dhanuṣā vidhyati*	*(karaṇa)*
C.	*dhanuḥ vidhyati*	*(kartṛ)*

By rule-ordering, the last of these would prevail over the first two. Cardona (1974) has not raised this question, but it is an important question. We in fact may have to question both the wider scope of rule-ordering as accepted in the View [A], and also the notion that each *kāraka* is simultaneously both dependent and independent. One suspects that probably neither of these two notions are historically Pāṇinian. Pāṇini, trying to distinguish his *kartṛ* from other *kārakas* says that *kartṛ* is that which is *svatantra* "independent", implying that all other *kārakas* are *paratantra* "dependent". If, now one accepts the new conception developed by Kātyāyana and Patañjali that each *kāraka* is independent with respect to its own action, but is dependent with respect to the main action, then one is forced to bring in some additional notions such as the main action *(pradhāna-kriyā)* and the subordinate actions *(gauṇa-kriyā)*. Without these and some other conceptions, one cannot resolve the derivational problems posed above. Pāṇini does not have any of this additional terminology in his grammar. Hence, it is very unlikely that Pāṇini, himself held this conception. Rich as this newer conception is, it is not Pāṇinian, and hence Pāṇini's grammar does not have to be answerable to problems created by this later conception. Thus both the problem and the basis on which it has been predicated in View [B] are in all probability un-Pāṇinian.

The fundamental logic of Pāṇinian definitions of *kārakas* may be briefly stated in the following way. P.1.4.54. *(svatantraḥ kartā)* says that among all factors contributing to bring about an action, that one which is independent is termed *kartṛ* "agent". The basic implications of this rule may be stated as follows. Among all different factors contributing to bring about an action, at any given time there can be only one factor which can be viewed as being independent. All other factors must be dependent factors. Also, no factor can at the same time be both dependent and independent with respect to the same action. Thus, this basic logic would preclude any factor being simultaneously classified in two ways. Thus, the same thing cannot simultaneously be both the object and the agent of the same action. It is interesting to note that the wording of the rule P.3.1.87 *(karmavat karmaṇā tulyakriyaḥ)* also lends support to such a conclusion. This rule allows the derivation of the so called *karma· kartṛ* or reflexive passive construction such as *odanaḥ pacyate* "rice cooks (itself)". In such a construction, Pāṇini believes that "rice" is the agent of the verb *pacyate* "cooks". However, this agent, being reflexive, has a relation to the action of cooking which is similar to that of an object *(karma)*. Under such circumstances, Pāṇini says that this object-like agent requires passive morphology for the active verb. The interesting point is that Pāṇini does not say that here is an agent which is at the same time an object. There is no such notion of agent-object identity in Pāṇini's grammar as claimed by S. D. Joshi. That is why Pāṇini speaks of an agent which is *like* an object in some ways, but not of an agent which *is* at the same time an object. As we shall see, this kind of an issue is ultimately determined in terms of a person's *vivakṣā* "intention". For a detailed discussion of the syntax of the *karma-kartṛ* construction, see my book *Ellipsis and Syntactic Overlapping : Current Issues in the Pānian Syntactic Theory*, Bhandarkar Oriental Research Institute, Poona, (1985).

VIEW [C] : SIMULTANEOUS MULTIPLE ONTOLOGICAL CLASSIFICATIONS FILTERED THROUGH THE SPEAKER'S INTENTIONALITY : *ONLY ONE CLASSIFICATION INTENDED AT A TIME*

To answer the problem as stated in View [B] above, Kātyāyana and Patañjali propose to filter the multiple ontological classifications for a given *kāraka* through the screen of the speaker's intention *(vivakṣā)*. They use the notion *vivakṣā* as a solution to problems, rather than as a source of problems. Below we shall examine the two contexts where Kātyāyana and Patañjali use the notion of *vivakṣā* to solve problems created by multiple classifications and rule-ordering. At the same time they use the notion of *vivakṣā* in two different ways, indicating that they themselves do not yet have a fully consolidated notion of *vivakṣā* and its role in the Pāṇinian system as perceived by them.

Kātyāyana's *Vārttika* 15 on P.1.4.23 says[11]: "That is not the problem, because each *kāraka* is both dependent and independent, and hence these aspects would be wished to be expressed in alternative ways, and based on this wish to express there will be the appropriate designation." It should be noted that Kātyāyana does not use the term *vivakṣā* in this *Vārttika,* but the uses the term *vacana* "expression". Using the notion of *vvivakṣā,* Patañjali says[12]: "In every case, the independence (of a *kāraka* with respect to its own action) and dependence (of a *kāraka* with respect to the action of the main agent) are both intended *(vivakṣitam)*. These will be expressed in alternative ways *(tayoḥ paryāyena vacanam)*. Depending on which one is to be expressed, there will be the appropriate designation *(vacanāśrayā ca samjnā)*."

Here for the first Patañjali is talking about not just simultaneous multiple ontological classifications, but simultaneously *intended* multiple ontological classifications. Of course in this case, these are truly not contradictory to each other — but they are apparently deemed to be so in this argument. I have expressed my view that these notions of a *kāraka* being independent in terms of its own action and dependent in terms of the action of the main agent are most likely not historically Pāṇinian notions. Even assuming these notions, Kātyāyana and Patañjali do not resolve the problem by using P.1.4.1-2. These rules are the actual cause of their problem. The problem is resolved not by making one classification prevail over the other by rule-ordering, but by allowing alternative ways of expression — something that we are told by Cardona and Joshi-Roodbergen Pāṇini, meant to prevent by his rules P.1.4.1-2. Once we are allowed alternative ways of expressing each of the two classifications, there is no question of rule ordering being a problem. This argument is designed to by-pass the problem posed by rule-ordering. There is also a further subtle distinction made here by Patañjali. He says that both the classifications — dependence and independence — are simultaneously intended, but expressed in alternative ways. This means that here the term *vivakṣā* is used not so much to mean "the speaker's intention to express something", but to mean a kind of express acknowledgement of the inevitable co-existence of these two classifications on the part of the speaker, but he does not and cannot intend to express these two classifications simultaneously. These two phases may be labelled *vivakṣā* (1) and *vivakṣā* (2). The first is acknowledgement on the part of the speaker of the multiple possibilities, while the second is the particular intention to express a particular selection of meaning.

Kātyāyana and Patañjali use *vivakṣā* "speaker's intention" as a means to get out of problems created by multiple ontological or logical classifications and rule-ordering. An important argument is presented in the *Vārttikas* 4-5 on P.1.4.23 and the *Mahābhāṣya* on these *Vārttikas*.[13] Kātyāyana and Patañjali deal with the following examples:

[D] *vṛkṣasya parṇam patati* "The leaf of the tree falls."
[E] *vṛkṣāt parṇam patati* "The leaf falls from the tree."

The general larger argument is as follows. If one does not properly restrict the scope of the term *kāraka* as it occurs in P.1.4.23 *(kārake)*, then according to Kātyāyana and Patañjali, items whether they are related or unrelated to actions will get the specific designations. Thus, while describing a situation where a leaf of a tree falls from that tree, one would have to consider that tree both as being a point of departure *(apāye dhruvam)* and an entity related to the leaf. Thus, given the possible conflict of these two classifications — *kāraka* and non-*kāraka* classifications —, the *kāraka* classification would prevail over the non-*kāraka* classification. Thus, one would be able to get only the ablative construction [E], and one would not be able to derive the genitive construction [D]. The force of the argument is that this situation would occur simply on the basis of the existence of the multiple ontological classifications, irrespective of one's intention.

To answer this difficulty, Kātyāyana and Patañjali bring in the notion of *vivakṣā* "speaker's intention". They argue that if one wants to express the semantic message of the construction [D], then one does not intend to express the fact that the tree is the point of departure. The only intended fact is that of the leaf being related to that tree. Therefore, while there may be many simultaneous ontological classifications possible in the objective reality, the language expresses only a subjective selection out of such possibilities, and therefore there will not be a problem. Patanjali says[14]: "There is no problem (in the construction [D]). Why ? Because the notion of the departure (of the leaf from the tree) is not intended to be expressed. Then what (is intended to be expresed) ? (Just) the relationship (between the leaf and the tree). When the notion of the departure (of the leaf from the tree) is intended to be expressed, then there indeed is the designation *apādāna* (for the tree) as in construction [E]. At that time the relationship (between the leaf and the tree) is not intended to be expressed."

This is a very instructive passage. Here, the difficulty has been created because of the existence of purely ontological multiple classifications which exist irrespective of one's intention to express them. The notion of rule-ordering is not brought up in this particular case. However, the solution to the difficulty has been offered by placing a higher value on the intentionality of the speaker than on the ontology of the objective world. The final claim of Kātyāyana and Patañjali is that it is the intention of the speaker that makes a choice between many objectively and subjectively available alternative classifications for a given item. This principle of intentional choice is the solution to problems created by other principles such as rule-ordering and purely ontological multiple classifications. This *vivakṣā* is not the *vivakṣā* (1) or the acknowledgement of the existence of ontological classifications. It is the *vivakṣā* (2) or the particular intention to express a particular selection of meaning.

The previous studies of this area of Pāṇini's syntax have created an impression that there is a consolidated view represented in the works of Kātyāyana and Patañjali. In the opinion of these previous studies, the speaker's intention is the cause of the problem of simultaneous multiple classifications and to resolve this problem, Pāṇini built his rule-ordering procedure P.1.4.1-2.

The analysis in this paper points to a very different situation. There is no single consolidated position in the words of Kātyāyana or Patañjali. We can discern at least three distinct sets of arguments in their works. In their works, it is abundantly clear that they make at least three different levels of classifications :

PURELY ONTOLOGICAL OR LOGICAL MULTIPLE CLASSIFICATIONS

SPEAKER'S INTENTION

Vivakṣā (1) : Acknowledgement of Multiple Ontological Classifications

Vivakṣā (2) : Specific Intention To Express A Specific Classification — Ontological Or Otherwise

On the basis of the above discussion, can we posit a Pāṇinian alternative ? This is a difficult choice. As pointed out earlier, it is most unlikely that Pāṇini himself had the conception of each *kāraka* being simultaneously dependent and independent and hence simultaneously liable to two classifications. Since these notions have no likely basis in Pāṇini's grammar, the problems raised in the works of Kātyāyana and

Patañjali are not really applicable to Pāṇini grammar. Going back to View [*A*], the main problem with it is that it assumes that at any one time we can consider only two possible classifications. Thus, in dealing with examples A (**dhanuṣaḥ vidhyati*) and B (*dhanuṣā vidhyati*), it is claimed that P.1.4.1-2 allow us to retain the latter classification of the bow as an instrument, and allow us to prevent the classification as a point of departure. But in the same vein, it is claimed that among the constructions A (**dhanuṣaḥ vidhyati*) and C (*dhanuḥ vidhyati*), P.1.4.1-2 allow us to retain C and prevent A. This is because the classification of the bow as *kartṛ* "agent" is later than its classification as *apādāna* "point of departure".

A simple argument can prove the folly of this above claim. If P.1.4.1-2 function with respect to the examples A and B taken as a pair, and if they also function with respect to A and C taken as a pair, what is there to prevent these rules to function with respect to all the examples A, B and C taken together ? If we do that, then C will prevail over both A and B and we would not be able to derive the construction B, which by all indications is an acceptable construction. There is nothing in Pāṇini's grammar to indicate that multiple ontological classifications come only in pairs, (and even if they did, we still have the pair [B] + [C]). These multiple ontological classifications, unchecked by the speaker's intention, can exist not just in pairs but in all their imaginable multiplicity. In that case, only the last classification *kartṛ* "agent" will survive for the *kārakas*. Among arguments grouped under View [B] above, Kātyāyana and Patañjali do in fact raise a similar objection to the unwanted results of rule-ordering being combined with multiple classifications. Their objection may be based on slightly different ontology of *kārakas*, but the objection would apply to View [A] nevertheless.

This makes it clear that one cannot simply have a multiplicity of purely ontological classifications checked simply by the device of rule-ordering in P.1.4.1-2. The only other likely principle that comes into the picture, and has been used by Kātyāyana and Patañjali to solve these problems, is that of *vivakṣā* "speaker's desire". This principle of *vivakṣā* claims that while there may exist many possible subjective and objective classifications for a given item, the speaker intends to express a particular selection from among these possibilities. This freedom of the speaker has been acknowledged in the system of Pāṇini. As I pointed out in Deshpande (1979: 142-3): "Pāṇini's grammar presupposes a certain concept of *vivakṣā*, 'speaker's desire', and it is not an automation which can produce a text on its own. Who should decide whether the grammar should produce *gantum icchati* or *jigamiṣati ?* Given the rule that a verbal inflection may express agent, object or action (ref : P.3.4.69), who is to decide whether the grammar should produce *rāmo gacchati* or *rāmeṇa gamyate.* The fact is that in Pāṇini's grammar certain operations are involuntary and do not require any input from the 'user', while there are a great deal of operations which tacitly require the voluntary decision and choice of the 'user' . . . . Thus the well-known grammatical maxim *vivakṣātaḥ k ārakāṇi bhavanti* 'the *kārakas* are dependent on the speaker's desire is not meant to replace the automatic operations in Pāṇini's grammar, but to indicate the source of input for the voluntary operations." Thus, contrary to the conclusions of previous scholars, the speakers' desire is the solution to the problems created by multiple classifications and rule-ordering, and not vice-versa.

If it is the speaker's intention that decides whether one wants to express the bow as an instrument or the agent of the act of shooting, then what is the purpose of rule-ordering prescribed by P.1.4.1-2? If the argument in favour of *vivakṣā* makes this procedure of rule-ordering vacuous, then one would have to say : *siddhyati evam, apāṇinīyaṁ tu bhavati* "The results are accomplished in this manner, but the procedure becomes un-Pāṇinian".

Rule-ordering as stated by P.1.4.1-2 is certainly not without a purpose, but one need not impute into Pāṇini a global ordering of conceptual categories to justify the existence of P.1.4.1-2. There are many other qualitatively different examples in Pāṇini's *Aṣṭadhyāyi* to illustrate the purpose of this rule-ordering. For instance, consider the example [F] below :

[F] *grāmam adhiśete* "X lives in a village. In Pāṇini's conception, the village is the locus (*ādhara*) of the action of dwelling and hence by the normal rule P.1.4.45 (*ādhāro' dhikaraṇam*), the village would get the *kāraka* designation *adhikaraṇa*. However, P.1.4.46 *(adhi-śīṅ-sthāsāṁ karma)* says that the locus in the case of verbs such as *adhi śi* gets the designation *karma*. Then by P.1.4.1-2, P.1.4.46 prevails over P.1.4.45, and hence one is allowed to derive the desired accusative usage [F], and prevent what would otherwise have been a locative usage. (This problem cannot be resolved by the general principles of *utsarga* 'general' and *apavāda* 'exception' rules, because as Kātyāyana notes in his *Vārttika (anyatra saṁjnāveśāt niyamārthaṁ vacanam)* on P.1.4.1, Pāṇini needs the multiplicity of designations for a given item elsewhere in his grammar. The section headed by P.1.4.1-2 is an exception to the general procedures.) Here, there is no multiplicity of intentional or even ontological classifications, but only a multiplicity of grammatical classifications and expressions. Pāṇini's rule-ordering, in this case, controls neither the intentional nor ontological multiplicity, but only a multiplicity of grammatical designations.

Finally, one may conclude that intentionality as far as it relates to semantic categories is not controlled by Pāṇini through rule-ordering (P.1.4.1-2). Multiplicity of intended simultaneous semantic classifications is not anticipated by Pāṇini, except in complex sentences such as causative constructions. However, given a particular choice of intended meaning, Pāṇini's grammar does sometimes anticipate a multiplicity of possible expressions, sometimes desirable as in the case of P.1.4.43 *(divaaḥ karma ca)*, and sometimes undersirable as in the case of P.1.4.46 *(adhi-śīṅ–sthāsāṁ karma)*. Where the multiplicity of possible expression is desirable, Pāṇini makes use of inclusive devices such as *ca* "and" in P.1.4.43, which allows the same item to have two grammatical designations, or the ascription of two alternative case-endings to express a given grammatical category such as in P.2.3.12 *(gaty-artha-karmaṇi dvitīyācaturthyau ceṣṭāyām-anadhvani)* which allows the *karma* "object" of verbs of motion to be expressed either with the accusative or dative endings, under certain conditions. Here, there is no multiplicity of intended meanings or of grammatical designations, but only of surface expressions. Where

Pāṇini wishes to prevent the multiplicity of surface-expressions, which he fears is likely to result because of two or more possible grammatical designations — not intended meanings — he uses the device of rule-ordering to prevent the former by allowing the latter categories to prevail over the former. Thus, the rule-ordering device of P.1.4.1-2 remains significant even after rejecting the claims made in earlier Pāṇinian scholarhip for its use to control the supposed multiplicity of intended meanings.

NOTES AND REFERENCES

1. There are good examples in the tradition of Sanskrit grammarians in which mutually incompatible alternatives are both used depending upon the need of a given occasion. The "Two Methods of Interpeting Pāṇini", i.e. the *yathoddeśapakṣa* and the *kāryakālapakṣa* have been both retained by the tradition. See S. D. Joshi (1965). Joshi-Roodbergen (1980 : i. vi) discuss the two mutually exclusive views about the derivational process, i.e. *vākyasaṁskārapakṣa* and *padasaṁskārapakṣa*. While discussing the purposes of studying Pāṇini's grammar, Patañjali *Mahābhāṣya*, Vol. I, pp. 2-4) refers to both the derivational ability as well as the interpretive ability to be gained by studying Pāṇini's grammar.
2. It is customary to say that there are six *kārakas*. Such a statement must be understood as referring not to the roles, but to the *kāraka* designations. There are twenty rules ascribing particular *kāraka* designations to particular semantic roles (P.1.4.24-44), but there are only six *kāraka* designations (seven, if one includes *hetu* as a separate term). Thus, it is clear that there are more semantic categories than the syntactic designations.
3. The Pāṇinian grammarians do not specifically argue that the *kāraka* roles and designations are language-specific. They are, however, interested only in dealing with Sanskrit.
4. For instance, the *vārttika* quoted by Patañjali on P.1.4.2 *(Mahābhāṣya*, Vol. I, p. 322) says : *supāṁ karmādayo' py arthāḥ* "The case-endings *(sup)* have even the *karma* etc. as their meanings." Occasionally one does find a careful statement in the traditional literature. For instance, Śabara in his '*Mīmāṁsā sūtra-bhāṣya* (Pt. I, p. 408) says : *dvitīyā-vibhaktih kartur īpsitatame varttate*, "The second case occurs to express that which is most desired to be accomplished by the agent." Here, instead of using the word *karma* to refer to the meaning of the accusative case-endings, Śabara explicitly uses the semantic role. But Pāṇini himself is not free from such usage of mixed levels of terminology. In defining the designation *karma*, Pāṇini says : *kartur īpstitatamaṁ karma* (P.1.4.49). Here, the expression for the semantic role, i.e. *kartur īpsitatamam* already uses the syntactic designation *kartṛ*, rather than using the semantic term *svatantra*. Thus, this mixing of terminology is very wide-spread. Agreeing with Ananthanarayana (1970) that there is *terminological confusion* in Pāṇini's grammar, Dipti Sharma (1975 : 114)

cites P.1.4.46 *(adhiśīn-sthāsāṁ karma)* and says that here Pāṇini used the *kāraka* term *karma* instead of using the case term *dvitīyā*. I think this is not an appropriate example. She is hereself not very sure about this example (cf. p. 141-142). Because of P.1.4.46 as it is, these verbs become *sakarmaka* and can have regular passives, which would not be possible with the word *dvitīyā*.

5. *kim punāḥ dravyaṁ sādhanam āhosvid guṇaḥ/ . . . guṇa ity āha/ kathaṁ jñāyate/ evaṁ hi kaścit kañcit pṛcchati — kva devadatta — iti / sa tasmāy ācaste — asau vṛkṣe — iti / — kātarsmin — / yas tiṣṭhati — iti / sa vṛkso' dhikaraṇam bhūtvānyena śabdenābhisambadhyamānaḥ kartā sampadyate / dravye punh sādhane sati yat karma karmaiva syāt . . . .yad adhikaraṇam adhikaraṇam eva / Mahābhāṣya*, on P.2.3.1., Vol. I, p. 442.
6. For a discussion of this point in connection with modern case-grammars, see : Stanley Starosta (1982 : 3ff).
7. For a critique of Joshi-Roodbergen (1975) view of Candragomin's syntax, see Deshpande (1979).
8. *apādānam uttarāṇi dhanuṣā vidhyati kaṁsapātryām bhuṅkte gāṁ doghi dhanur vidhyatīti (Vārttika 30), karaṇam parāṇi sādhv asiś chinatti (Vārttika 33), adhikaraṇaṁ karma geham praviśati (Vārttika 33), adhikaraṇaṁ kartā sthālī pacati (Vārttika 34), Mahābhāṣya*, Vol. I, pp. 303-3.
9. *siddhaṁ tu pratikṁrakaṁ kriyābhedāt pacādīnāṁ karaṇādhikaraṇayoḥ, kartṛbhā vaḥ Vārttika* 7 on P.1.4.23, *Mahābhāṣya*, Vol. I, p. 324.
10. *apadanadinaṁ to aprasiddhih, Varttika* 14 on P.1.4.23 *saṁjñāyāā aprasiddhih / yavata sarvatraiva svatantryain vidyate paratantryain ca tatra paratlvat-Kartṛsaṁjñaiva prāpnoti/, Mahābhāṣya*, Vol. I, p. 325.
11. *na vā svatantra-paratantratvāt tayoḥ paryāyena vacanaṁ vacanāśrayā ca saṁjñā, Vārttika* 15 on P.1.4.23. *Mahābhāṣya*, Vol. I, p. 325.
12. *sarvatraiva svātantryam pāratantryaṁ ca vivakṣitam / . . . tayoḥ sv\o(a,¯)tantryap\o(a,¯)ratantryayo\o(h,̣) pary\o(a,¯)ye\o(n,̣)a cacanam bhaviṣyati/ vacanāśrayā ca saṁjnā bhaviṣyati/, Mahābhāṣya*, Vol. I, p. 325.
13. *apādānaṁ ca uṛkṣasya parṇam patatīti/, Vārttika* 4 on P.1.4.23, *apādāna-saṁjñā ca prāpnoti/ kva/ vṛkṣasya parṇam patatīti/, Mahābhāṣya*, Vol. I, p. 323.
14. *na vā apayasyāvivakṣitatvāt, Vārttika* 5 on P.1.4.23. *na vā eṣa doṣaḥ/ kiṁ kāraṇam/ apāyasyāvivakṣitatvāt/ nātrāpāyo vivakṣitaḥ / kiṁ tarhi / sambandhaḥ / yadā ca āpāyo vivakṣito bhavati, bhavati tadāpādānasaṁjñā/ tad yathā aṛkṣāt parṇam patatīti/ sambandhas tu tadā na vivakṣito bhavati/, Mahābhāṣya*, Vol. I, p. 324.

BIBLIOGRAPHY

Ananthanarayana, H. S. 1970. "The Kāraka Theory and Case Grammar' *Indian Linguistics*, Vol. 31, pp. 14-27.

Bronkhorst, Johannes. 1979. "The Role of Meaning in Pāṇini's Grammar' *Indian Linguistics*, Vol. 40, No. 3, pp. 146-157.

Cardona, George. 1967. "Pāṇini's Syntactic Categories". *Journal of the Oriental Institute*, Baroda, Vol. 16, No. 3, pp. 201-215.

_______ . 1974. "Pāṇini's Kārakas : Agency, Animation and Identity". *Journal of Indian Philosophy*, Vol. 2, Nos. 3-4, pp. 231-306.

_______ . 1976. *Pāṇini : A Survey of Research*. The Hague-Paris : Mouton.

Deshpande, Madhav M. 1979. "Candragomin's Syntactic Rules : Some Misconceptions". *Indian Linguistics*, Vol. 40. pp. 133-145.

_______ . 1980. *Evolution of Syntactic Theory in Sanskrit Grammar: Syntax of the Sanskrit Infinitive-tum UN*. Ann Arbor : Karoma Publishers, Inc.

_______ . (1985). *Ellipsis and Syntactic Overlapping : Current Issues in the Paninian Syntactic Theory*. Bhandarkar Oriental Research Institute, Poona.

Joshi, S. D. 1965. "Two Methods of Interpretive Pāṇini". *Journal of the Univeristy of Poona*, Humanities Section. Vol. 23, pp. 53-61.

_______ . 1974. "Pāṇini's Treatment of Kāraka Relations". *Charudeva Shastri Felicitation Volume*. Delhi. pp. 258-270.

Joshi, S. D. and Roodbergen J.A.F. 1975. Patañjali's *Vyākaraṇa-Mahābhāṣya, Kārakāhnika*. With Introduction, Translation, and Notes. Publications of the Centre of Advanced Study in Sanskrit, Class C. No. 10. Poona : Univeristy of Poona.

_______ . 1980 Patañjali's *Vyākaraṇa-Mahābhāṣya, Vibhaktyāhnika*. With Introduction. Translation, and Notes. Publications of the Centre of Advanced Study in Sanskrit, Class C, No. 12. Poona : University of Poona.

Kiparsky, Paul 1982. *Some Theoretical Problems in Pāṇini's Grammar*. Post-Graduate and Research Department Series. No. 16. Poona : Bhandarkar Oriental Institute.

Kiparsky, Paul and J. F. Staal. 1969. "Syntactic and Semantic Relations in Pāṇini" *Foundations of Language*, Vol. 5, pp. 83-117.

Mīmāṁsā-sūtras of Jaimini. With Śabara's *Bhāṣya* and Kumārila's *Tantravārttika* and *Ṭupṭīkā*. In six parts. Anandashrama Sanskrit Series 97. Poona. 1929.

Sharma, Dipti, 1975. *Vyākaraṇik Koṭiyo kā Viśleṣaṇātmak Adhyayan* (in Hindi). Patna : Bihar Hindi Granth Academy.

Starosta, Stanley. 1982. "Case-Relations, Perspective, and Patient Centrality". *University of Hawaii Working Papers in Linguistics*, Vol. 14, pp. 1-33.

Van Nooten, Barend A. 1969. "Pāṇini's Theory of Verbal Meaning". *Foundations of Language*, Vol. 5, No. 2, pp. 242-255.

Vyākaraṇa–Mahābhāṣya of Patañjali Edited by F. Kielhorn. 3rd edition by K. V. Abhyankar. In three volumes. 1962, 1965 and 1972. Poona : Bhandarkar Oriental Research Institute.

Cardona, George. 1967. "Pāṇini's Syntactic Categories", *Journal of the Oriental Institute* (Baroda), Vol. 16, No. 3, pp. 201-215.

——— 1974. "Pāṇini's Kārakas: Agency, Animation and Identity", *Journal of Indian Philosophy*, Vol. 2, Nos. 3-4, pp. 231-306.

——— 1976. *Pāṇini: A Survey of Research*. The Hague-Paris: Mouton.

Deshpande, Madhav M. 1979. "Subordination & Syntactic Rules: Some Misconceptions", *Indian Linguistics*, Vol. 40, pp. 133-145.

——— 1980. *Evolution of Syntactic Theory in Sanskrit Grammar: Syntax of the Sanskrit Infinitive -tumUN*. Ann Arbor: Karoma Publishers, Inc.

——— 1985. *Ellipsis and Syntactic Overlapping: Current Issues in Pāṇinian Syntactic Theory*. Bhandarkar Oriental Research Institute, Poona.

Joshi, S. D. 1966. "Two Methods of Interpretation", *Journal of the University of Poona*, Humanities Section, Vol. 25, pp. 53-61.

——— 1974. "Pāṇini's Treatment of Kāraka Relations", *Charudeva Shastri Felicitation Volume*, Delhi, pp. 258-270.

Joshi, S. D. and Roodbergen, J. A. F. 1975. *Patañjali's Vyākaraṇa-Mahābhāṣya, Kārakāhnika. With Introduction, Translation and Notes*. Publications of the Centre of Advanced Study in Sanskrit, Class C, No. 10. Poona: University of Poona.

——— 1986. *Patañjali's Vyākaraṇa-Mahābhāṣya, Paspaśāhnika. With Introduction, Translation and Notes*. Publications of the Centre of Advanced Study in Sanskrit, Class C, No. 15. Poona: University of Poona.

Kiparsky, Paul 1982. *Some Theoretical Problems in Pāṇini's Grammar*. Post-Graduate and Research Department Series No. 16. Poona: Bhandarkar Oriental Research Institute.

Kiparsky, Paul and J. F. Staal 1969. "Syntactic and Semantic Relations in Pāṇini", *Foundations of Language*, Vol. 5, pp. 83-117.

Mahābhāṣya of Patañjali. With Kaiyaṭa's *Pradīpa* and Nāgeśa's *Uddyota* [illegible] Sanskrit Series 97, [illegible].

[illegible] 197? *[illegible]*. Patna: Bihar Hindi Grantha Academy.

Saroja, [illegible] 1982. "[illegible] and Pāṇini", [illegible] *Papers in Linguistics*, Vol. 14, pp. 1-73.

Van Nooten, Barend A. 1969. "Pāṇini's Theory of Verbal Meaning", *Foundations of Language*, Vol. 5, No. 2, pp. 242-255.

Vasu, S. C. *Siddhānta Kaumudī of Bhaṭṭoji Dīkṣita*. Edited and Translated into English in three volumes. Delhi, 1962 and 1982. [illegible]

Section B
Sanskrit Literature

5

An Old View on Rasavadalankāra *

PRATAP BANDYOPADHYAY

It is well known that the figures of speech headed by *rasavat* in Sanskrit poetics consist in the delineation of *rasa* (aesthetic relish) and its varieties according to the old school of critics and in the subordination of the same to another idea (another *rasa* or the like, to be more precise) according to the new school.[1] Apart from this development of the conception of these figures, there is a peculiar view on the same noted and rejected by critics like Ānandavardhana and Kuntaka. Ānandavardhana cities the view thus :

> *cetanānāaṁ vāktyārthībhāvo rasādyalaṅkārasya viṣayaḥ*[2]
> (The treatment of sentient beings comes under the purview of the figures of speech *rasavat* etc.)

Kuntaka is clearer in his presentation :

> *athavā cetanapadārthagocaratayā rasavadalaṅkārasya niścetana-vastuviṣayatvena copamadīnāṃ viṣayavibhāgo vyavasthāpyate*[3] (Or a distinction between the figure *rasavat* on the one hand and simile etc. on the other hand is made by taking the former as connected with sentient beings and the latter with insentient objects).

According to his view, the treatment of sentient beings makes *rasavat* or the like and that of the insentient makes *upamā* and other *alaṅkāras*. It is not clear how the *alaṅkāras rasavat, preyas, ūrjasvin samāhita*, etc. would mutually differ according to the holder of this view.

Ānandavardhana proceeds to criticize the view as follows. If *rasavat* etc. consist in the treatment of the sentient, *upamā* etc. would be left with very little scope or hardly any scope at all. For, even when the behaviour of the insentient is the main theme, the description of the sentient will be associated with it somehow or other :

> *tarhy upamādīnāṃ praviralaviṣayatā nirviṣayatā vābhihitā syāt/vasmād acetanavastnvrtee vākyārthībhīte Punśa cetana-vastu vrttāntayojanayā yathākathaṅcid bhavitavyaṁ*[4]

The word *yathākathañcit* has been explained in the *Locana* as *vibhāvādirūpatayā*.[5] (as *vibhāva* etc. of a particular rasa. In other words, even when the theme is the description of insentient beings, reference to sentient begins comes in as *uddīpanavibhāva* (the exciting condition of aesthetic relish). If it be still maintained that when the description of the insentient is the main theme, there should be no *rasavat* (in spite of association of the sentient with it), a bulk of literary productions will have to be called *nirasa*, i.e., bereft of aesthetic relish :

> *atha satyām api tasyāṁ yatrācetanānām vākyārthībhāvo nāsau rasavadalaṅkārasya viṣaya ity ucyate tan mahataḥ kāvya-prabandhasya rasanidhānabhātasya abhihitaṁ sayāt*[6]

As examples Ānandavardhana cites three verses. The first one (from the Fourth Act of Kalidasa's *Vikramorvaśīya)* describes a river personified as Urvaśī. The second one (from the same source) describes a creeper, fancying it to be the speaker's beloved. The third one describes the withering creepers on the bank of the Yamunā which once witnessed the love-making of Rādhā and cowherdesses with Kṛṣṇa.[7] In all these examples, the description of the insentient is the main theme, but there is an association of the behaviour of the sentient as well. As per the above argument, these beautiful verses have to be declared *nīrasa.*

On the other hand, if it be contended that a case ot *rasavat* or the like is that where there is an association of the behaviour of the sentient (and, as such, the verses referred to above are instances of *rasavat*), *alaṅkāras* like *upamā* will have no scope left for them. For, there cannot be a case of the description of the insentient where the association of the behaviour of the sentient is totally lacking so as to make it an instance of *upamā* or some other *alaṅkāra*, but not *rasavat*. At least as *vibhāva* etc. the behaviour of the sentient would come in. So says Ānandavardhana :

> *atha yatra cetanavastuvṛttāntayojanāsti tatra rasādir alaṅkāraḥ/tad evaṁ saty upamādayo nirviṣayāḥ praviralaviṣayā va syuḥ/yasmān nāsty evāsāv acetanavastuvṛttānto yatra cetanavastuvṛttāntayojanā nāsty antato vibhāvatvena/*[8]

Kuntaka also refers to the view, as we have already noted, and criticizes the same in similar words :

> *tad api na vidvajjanāvarjanaṁ vidadhāti/ yasmād acetanānām api rasoddīpanasāmarthyasamucitasatkavisamullikhitasaukumāryasarasa tvād upamādīnāṁ praviralaviṣayatā nirviṣayatvaṁ vā syād iti śṛṅgārādirasanisyandasundarasya satkavipravāhasya ca nīrasatvaṁ prasajyata iti pratipāditam eva pūrvasūribhiḥ/*[9]

The *pūrvasūr is* referred to by Kuntaka obviously include Ānandavardhana, whose arguments he reproduces here.

It may be noted that no distinction between *rasa* and *rasavadalaṅkāra* has been made by the critics of the view in question. To deny *rasavat* in a given example is to call it devoid of *rasa* according to the criticism reproduced above. This is because with the old critics the conception of the subordination of sentiments, propounded later by Ānandavardhana,[10] had not developed. Bhaṁaha, Daṇḍin and Udbhaṭa define *rasavat* as delineation of one of the *rasas*.[11] Ānandavardhana has taken up here the position of the old critics themselves in levelling his criticism against the old view on *rasavat* in question. It may appear, however, too much to contend, as does Ānandavardhana, that even when the description of the insentient is the main theme, the behaviour of the sentient would necessarily creep in. There may be *upamā* etc. involving the description of insentient objects exclusively. Possibly Ānandavardhana is here speaking of the whole works of renowned writers delineating *rasas* and not portions thereof where *upamā* etc. occur. Needless to say that for Ānandavardhana, the so-called *citrakāvya* or portrait with the delineation of *rasa* is not to be called poetry at all.[12] At any rate, Ānandavardhana was not in a position to accept the above view on *rasavat* etc., as the discovered a completely different conception of these *alanbāras* consisting in the subordination of *rasa* or the like, as stated in *karikā* II. 5 of the *Dhvanyaloka*, so vitally related to the concept of the *guṇībhūtavyanigya* variety of *kāvya* of the new school of critics.

It is not known who propounded the view in question or whether Ānandavardhana was the first person to reject it Śrīdhara, commentator of Mammaṭa's *Kāvyaprakāśa*, attributes it to Udbhaṭa when he reproduces the whole issue in the following words :

> *evam udbhaṭenāpi yatra cetanānāṁ vākyārthībhāvaḥ sa rasavadādyalaṅkārasya vīṣaya iti yad uktaṁ tad api na samyak upamādīnāṃ praviralaviṣayatvāpstteḥ/yato rāmādicaritavarnamayaṁ kāvyaṁ tatra copamadyaḥ santo 'pi na pṛthak sattāṁ labdhum kṣamā 'bhaveyuḥ rasavadādyalaṅkārair eva kvyasya spastīkārāt/ acetaṇa-varṇane tu kvacit sambhavāt yadi vā nirviṣavataiva teṣām syāt vasmād yatrāpy acetanānāṁ vā rasavādādyekārthībhāvas tatrāpi yathākathān cic caitanyādhyāropāc cetanavṛttāntayojanayā bhavitavyam eva taṭaś catiamādīnām viṣaye sarvatra rasavadādeh sāmrajyam iti/ athavā pāramārthikacetanānāṁ bhāvo rasavadāder visayo na tv adhyāropitacaitām ity ucyate tadānīm rasanidhānabhūtasya kāvyaprabandhasya nīrasatvam abhyupagtaṁ syāt'*[13]

(So also the statement of Udbhaṭa, viz., that it comes under the purview of embellishments like *rasavat* where the treatment of sentient beings is the theme, is not correct. For, this would leave very little scope for *simile* etc. Where a literary work consists in the account of the lives of Rāma and the like, simile etc., though present, cannot attain a separate position, since the literary appeal depends on embellishments like *resavat*. On the other hand, in the case of the description of insentient beings, which may sometimes take place, there is no scope for them, i.e. simile etc. For, even where the treatment of the insentient coexists with *rasavat* etc. there also must be association of the behaviour of the sentient somehow by virtue of super-imposition of consciousness on the former. Thus, *rasavat* etc. are always predominant in the realm of simile etc. If it be argued, on the contrary, the *rasavat* etc. have their scope in the case of actually sentient beings and not of those with consciousness superimposed on them, literary products which are treasures of *rasas* have to be admitted as bereft aesthetic charm.)

No such view is traceable in the *Kāvyālaṅkārasārasaṅgraha* of Udhaṭa. It might have been there in his *Bhāmahavivaraṇa*, a commentary on Bhāmaha's *Kāvyālaṅlara*. as indicated by Professor Sivaprasad Bhattacharya in his edition of Śrīdhara's commentary.[14] In all probability, the view is not Udbhaṭa's own. Had it been so, he would have recorded it in his original work *Kāvyālaṅkārasārasaṅgraha*, which deals with *alaṅkāras* exclusively. It is noteworthy, if Srīdhara's text be correct, that the view was known to an old critic like Udbhaṭa, and its antiquity, therefore, can be easily surmised.

The dichotomy *cetanānāṁ vākyārthībhāvah* and *acetanānāṁ Vākyārthībhāvaḥ* (*viṣayavibhāgaḥ*, as Kuntaka puts it), giving rise to *rasavat*, or *rasokti* as Bhoja would call it, on the one hand and *upamā* etc on the other, would remind us of Daṇḍin's dichotomy *svabhāvokti* and *vakrokti*.[15] Daṇḍin brings all literary embellishments, except *svabhāvokti*, under the category of *vakrokti*. This division, along with the one on the carpet, might have inspired Bhoja for his trichotomy — *vakrokti*, *svabhāvokti* and *rasokti* :

> *trividhaḥ khalv alaṅkaravargah — vakroktih svabhāvoktiḥ rasoktir iti/ tatropamādyalaṅkārapradhānye vakroktih śleṣādiguṇapradhānye svabhāvoktiḥ vibhāvānubhāvavyabhicārasaṁyogāt tu rasaniṣpattau rasoktir iti/*[16].

(embellishments are of three classes — figurative expression, natural expression and sentimential expression. Of these, figurative expression is that where figures of speech like simile are predominant; natural expression is that where literary excellences like harmony are predominant and sentimental expression is that where aesthetic relish is produced by means of the combination of stimuli, external manifestations and transitory moods.)

Though for Bhoja *rasokti* or *rasavat* was not *cetanānāṁ vākyārthibhāvaḥ* as discussed above, but identical with *rasa*, defined by Bharata as, *vibhāvānubhāvavyabhicārisaṁyogād rasaniṣpattiḥ*[17] (aesthetic relish is brought about by the combination of stimuli, external manifestations and transitory moods) and accepted, though variously interpreted, by later critics, he divided literary embellishments into three classes, of which according to him *rasa* was one. In other words, Bhoja's trichotomy might have been an amalgamation of the two dichotomies noted above with modification of the conception of *rasavat*. Bhoja did not submit to the concept of *rasavat* discussed above, but brought the generally accepted concept of *rasa* under the category of *alaṅkāra* and called it *rasokti* in order to bring it in line with Daṇḍin's *svabhāvokti* and *vakrokti*.

It is unfortunate that the critics who had occasion to refer to the above view on *rasavat* did not mention its source, while Śrīdhara's information in this regard, as we have seen above, is rather unreliable. Most probably the source book of this old view was lost before the advent of Ānandavardhana, who might have known it from an oral tradition or secondary sources accessible to him. If the original source be ever discovered, it may supply us with a missing link in the history of literary criticism in ancient India.

NOTES AND REFERENCES

*The kernel of the paper was presented in the Section on Classical Sanskrit of the XXXI Session of All-India Oriental Conference at Jaipur (India) in October 1982.

1. See Pratap Bandyopadhyay, 'The Figure of Speech *Udatta* in Sanskrit Poetics', *Bhāratibhānam (Light of Indology)* being Dr. K. V. Sarma Felicitation Volume, edited by S. Bhaskaran Nair, Panjab University Indological Series, Vishveshvaranand Visva Bandhu Institute of Sanskrit and Indological Studies, Panjab University, Hoshiarpur, 1989, pp. 236-42.
2. The *Dhvanyaloka* of Śri Ānandavardhānacārya with the *locana* and *Balapriya* Commentaries by Abhinavagupta and Rāmaśāraka and *Divyāñjana* Notes by Mahadeva Sastri, edited by Pattabhirama Sastri, Kashi Sanskrit Series 135, Chowkhamba Sanskrit Series Office, Banares City, 1940, under II.5, p. 198.

On the same view, see V. Raghavan, 'The Rasavadalamkara', *Professor M. Hiriyanna Birht Centenary Commemoration Volume* (1871-1971). edited by V. Raghavan and G. Marulasiddaiah : University of Mysore, Mysore, 1972. pp. 235-38 & 249-50.

3. *The Vakroktijīvita of Kuntaka*, Edited by K. Krishnamoorthy, Karnatak Univeristy, Dharwad, 1977, under III. II, p. 149, Ānandavardhana speaks of all the *alaṅkāras* headed by *rasavat*, whereas Kuntaka speaks of *rasavat* only, which, however, so far as this particular issue is concerned, may include other *alaṅkrā ras* of the class by *upalaksana* (implication of something in addition).
4. *Op. cit.*, p. 200.
5. p. 200. Later on the original text also has *antato vibhāvatvena* (pp. 200-204).
6. *Dhavnyāloka* II, pp. 200-201.
7. *Ibid.*, pp. 201-202.
8. *Ibid.*, pp. 201-204.
9. *Op. cit.*, p. 149.
10. *Op. cit.*, *II. 5 and virtti* theron.
11. *Kāvyālaṁkāra* of Bhāmaha (ed. by P. V. Naganatha Sastry, Wallace Printing House, Tanjore, editor's date 1927), III. 6; *Kāvyādarśa* of Dandin (ed. by Rangacharya Raddi Shastri, 2nd Ed., Government Oriental Series — Class A. No. 4, Bhandarkar Oriental Research Institute, Poona, 1970), II. 275. B, 280, 281; *Kāvyālaṅkārasārasaṁgraha* of Udbhata (with the Commentary *Laghuvṛtti* of Indurāja ed. by Narayana Daso Banhatti, First Ed., Bhandarkar Oriental Research Institute, Poona, 1925), IV. 3-4 and illustrative vs. IV. 2-4.
12. *See Dhvanyāloka*, III. 41 and *vṛitti* thereon : *tato'nyad rasabhāvāditātparyarahitaṁvyaṅgyārthaviśesaprakāśaktiśūnyaṁ ca kāvyaṁ kevalavācyavācakavaicitryamātaśrayenopanibaddham ālekhyaprakhyaṁ yad ābhāsate tac citram/ na tan mukhyaṁ kāvyam/ kāvyānukāro hy asu/*
13. The *Kāvyaprakāśa* of Mammata with the Commentary of Srīdhara (Part Two), edited by Sivaprasad Bhattacharya, Calcutta Sanskrit College Research Series No. XV. Text No. 10. Sanskrit College. Calcutta. 1961. Ch. V. pp. 141-42.
14. *Op. cit.*, p. 141. Udbhata wrote a commentary on Bharata's *Nāṭyasastra* also. But there was apparently little scope for making a reference to this view there.
15. *bhinnaṁ dividhā svchāvoktir vakroktiś ceti vāṅmayam/* - *Kavyādarśa*, II, 363. C-D.
16. Mahārāja Bhojarāja's *Sṛṅgāraprakāsa*, Second Volume, *Prakāśas* 9 to 14, Manuscripts collated by Yatiraja Swami of Malkote, revised and edited by G. R. Josyer, Coronation Press, Mysore, 1963, *Prakāśa 11* p. 438. Cf. *vakroktiś ca rasokitś ca svabhāvoktiś ca vānmayam* [— The *Saravatīkanthābharana* by Dhāreśvara Bhojadeva, with Commentaries of Rāmasimha (I-III) and Jagaddhara (IV). Edited by Kedarnatha Durgaprasad and Vasudev Laxman Sastri Pansikar, Kāvyamālā 95, Nirnaya-sagar Press, Bombay, 1925, V.8A-B. *Nāṭyaśastra* of Bharatamuni, with the Commentary *Abhinavabhāratī* of Abhinavaguptācarya, Vol. I. edited by Ramakrishna Kavi, Second Revised Edition by K. S. Ramaswami Sastri Siromani. Gaekwad's Oriental Series, No XXXVI, Oriental Institute, Baroda, 1956, Ch. p. 272.

6

'Gīta Govinda' and 'Song of Solomon'

JOHN B. ALPHONSO KARKALA

The two great love songs in world literature — The *Gīta Govinda* (Song of Govinda) and the *Song of Solomon* (variously titled as *Canticum Canticorum, Song of Songs which is Solomon's* or simply *Song of Solomon* or *Song of Songs*)[1] — are deeply embedded in the Hindu and Judaeo-Christian mystical traditions. While these poems have structured spiritual sensibilities within their respective traditions, both of them have been read outside their religious confines as great books among world classics, contributing to the multi-foliate human spiritual experience in unique ways. There are surprising similarities between them in spite of some obvious differences in detail of locale or language. However, what is of greater interest for us today is that both songs are not only intensely lyrical poems, but because of their verbal structure and design, poetic imagery and *dramatis personae* inlaid within mythic consciousness with symbolic suggestions, they could be examined from an aesthetic or literary point of view, in spite of their canonicity.

From the point of Comparative World Literature, both the *Gīta Govinda* and the *Song of Solomon* are essentially lyrical poems in their genesis, and in their imaginative re-organization of human experience, they are in the dramatic mode. They portray, like all other aesthetic verbal structures do, human emotions in intensely charged poetic imagery. The intensity comes from the fact that the central theme of the poem concentrates on the primordial creation re-enacted and recollected in the recreation in the human act of love. The narrative structure in both the poems is rather simple and direct, and does not need any great deal of elaboration. It can be understood in terms of a common structural pattern:

A Royal person sports with a large number of women given to love; they are lovers, wives or concubines. The experienced lover then chooses an inexperienced simple country girl as the beloved, takes her to a quiet green bower, and has a passionate encounter with her in the moonlight. After the affair, the lover goes away, leaving the girl bewildered. In her state of abandon, the beloved goes up and down the emotional scale experiencing anxiety, jealousy, suspicion, despair, longing, and fond recollection of the first love. The surrounding atmosphere also varies according to the beloved's moods and agony. In the night, the lover suddenly reappears. After initial sulking and coaxing, there is reconciliation and a description of the physical anatomy in concrete details. Finally, the lover and the beloved are drawn to each other unadorned, and surrender to a blissful union. When the passions are spent, the resolution comes when the lover and the beloved express to each other abiding love, loyalty, and unity.

With such a simple pastoral and romantic framework, the juicy poem should keep us awake for long at night and, in fact, these poems have kept awake many duellers with divinity in their long 'dark night of the soul'. The poems achieve extreme dramatic intensity in their rather chiselled statuesque images concentrated essentially in two characters, with a marginal background of a chorus of women and a confidante going in between. The *dramatis personae* in the poems could be compared for their striking similarities:

Gīta Govinda	**Song of Solomon**
12 Cantos	8 Chapters
KṚṢṆA, born a prince but his identity is hidden because he has been brought up secretly in a cowherd chief Nanda-Yaśodā family in Vrindāvan, on the banks of the river Jamuna. His identity is further	SOLOMON, King of Israel (state), by annointment, agent of good Yewehe, "husband of Israelis betrothed in steadfast love and faithfulness" (Hosea, 2 : 16-19). He is in the palace at the

masked because the prince-cum-shepherd Kṛṣṇa is also an incarnation of god Viṣnu, the preserver.	nation's capital in Jerusalem. The identity of the lover is thus masked by two-fold institutional positions.
RĀDHĀ, a cowherd country maid, chosen beloved of Kṛṣṇa. After the first encounter in a bower in the forest, is abandoned; she undergoes a variety of moods and emotions; she is coaxed to go to her lover. When the lover suddenly appears, she is reconciled and yields to him unadorned in ecstatic love. They vow abiding love and union.	SHULAMITE, a country maid, chosen beloved of Solomon, is brought to the palace garden. After the first encounter in the garden, the lover disappears. She undergoes a variety of emotions; she is coaxed to return to the lover. When the lover suddenly appears, she is reconciled and yields unadorned to ecstatic love, vowing abiding love and union.
GOPIS, cowherd women of Vrindāvan, gives to love-sport with Krishna.	Women-lovers, wives and concubines given to love-sport with Solomon.
Gopi, confidante of Radha who is a go-between of estranged Rādhā and Krishna.	Daughters of Jerusalem, a chorus, that appear to mediate between estranged Shulamite and Solomon.

Though no defence of the explicit love that is depicted in the *Gīta Govinda* and the *Song of Solomon* is needed, social attitudes to them have differed in their respective traditions. The manifestation of physical love is one of the four legitimate *Purusārthas* or Aims of life in the context of Indian spirituality : *Dharma* (law), *Artha* (well-being), *Kāma* (satisfaction of desires, including love) and *Mokṣā* (release or redemption). The pursuit of love of beauty and physical love, therefore, is a legitimate pursuit. Besides, the manifestation of physical love makes it possible, especially in Tantric tradition, and more generally in the context of Upanisadic union of Ātman-Brahman as a basis for transcendence to metaphysical or mystical union. The plurality of the perception of Truth makes such unifying vision essential and the transcendence is not obstructed by the duality. On the other hand, in the Judaeo-Christian traditions, the *Song of Solomon* had to contend with opponents and apologists. In the face of duality of Eros and Agape, profane and sacred love, the eroticism of the *Song of Solomon* remained problematic. A puritanic streak often contended that such explicit description of physical love is something less than sacred, and should be excluded from public readings in sacred portals. It was under such constraints that Edwin Arnold while translating the *Gīta Govinda* in the 19th century found it necessary to modify much, and completely omit the 12th canto of the *Gīta Govinda* from his translation, saying that its openness of love-making was too offensive to Western (or Victorian British) taste.[2]

In order to overcome such difficulties in dealing with the obvious sensuous eroticism of the *Song of Solomon*, Christian traditions have interpreted the *Song* as "an allegory of the love; of Jesus Christ for his bride, the Church" (Rev. 21 : 22, 9) and in the Judaic tradition it has been explained away as figurative of Lord Yewehe as the 'husband' of Israelis *(Hosea*, 2 : 16, 19).[3] The opposition to the inclusion of the *Song of Solomon* in the *Ketubin* (Writings) in the Hebrew *Holy Scriptures* was evident as early as the 1st century A.D. When the rabbinical congress was redacting canonical texts at the Council of Jamnia in Palestine in A.D. 90, in the face of fierce opposition to the *Song of Solomon*, Hebrew mystic Rabbi Akiba máde a passionate plea upholding the right of the *Song of Solomon* which is Holy of Holies.[4] We are fortunate that Rabbi Akiba's mystic vision persuaded and prevailed over the puritanical rejection of the *Song of Solomon*.

That brings us directly to the crucial mating imagery that is necessary to explain the culture cosmos and the two essential ingredients in it, namely the unknown beginning of the human condition by such archetypes as Yama-Yami or Adam-Lilith-Eve, and the unknown beginning of the universe in terms of two abstractions of feminine and masculine principles. These explanations are integrally rooted in the known imagery of creation in reference to human pair in the act of love-making, a biological prelude to pro-creation. Most culture traditions have adopted the mating imagery and its symbolic reference as the logic of mythic consciousness to explain the genesis of the universe. Thus, we have Father Heaven and Mother Earth mating to produce by their act of love the cosmic progeny of elemental creation. Verbally explained, that mating imagery appears and reappears in varying degrees of abstraction, but essentially remaining the element of eternal feminine and the eternal masculine principle : The Norse Divine Wind and Holy Water, the Semitic Elohim and Tiamat (Tehom, Gen. 1:2), the Hellenic Dark and the Deep, the Indic Purusa and Prakriti and the chakras of two inverted triangles of Kundalini Yoga, and the Chinese Yin and Yang of Tao.

The reality of primordial mating 'act' is the substance of spiritual 'fact' sustaining belief systems. They revive in our mythic consciousness the recollection of physical experience of loving. The verbal structure that induces the poetic imagery of two unadorned lovers in the dramatic encounter in a green bower under enticing moonlight, though suggests Eros in the primary level, provides the basis to grasp the primordial mating of the first creation by the divine act of love-making and cosmic genesis. Creativity as a feature of human life and human activity, be it biological or aesthetic creation, becomes a metaphor for divine or cosmic creation. It is argued by Northrop Frye that "we are free, upto a point, to shape our beliefs : what we are not free to do is to alter that is really a part of our cultural genetic code."[5]

Consequently, we are left with the choice of dual perceptions of two loving acts and their identification — conscious and unconscious — a perception of 'multeity in unity' as Coleridge characterized,[6] *e peluribus unum*. Mystics all over the world generally explain to us their visionary perception of the wave and ocean, the petal and flower at the same time without duality, and induce us to seek such transcending transformation for our redemption. Relative to the intensity of our own spiritual antenna, we may reach such awareness, reducing visuality to realized experience, thus participating whether consciously or unconsciously, in the primordial mating of cosmic creation. The aesthetic reintegration of that experience in the union of lovers and the dissolution of duality is perhaps what the Puruṣasukta in the *Ṛg Veda* reveals where the Sacrificer, the Sacrificee and the Sacrifice all become one.[7]

Whether we understand the cosmic creation in the process of Father Heaven or Mother Earth, etc., or whether we take the position that everything ultimately is One that is Tao, Brahman, or Spinoza's Metaphysical Substance, Einstein's Energy, or what contemporary astrophysicists call Singularity, in our approximation to Truth, we are willing to superimpose for our process of understanding the beginning and the end, creation and recreation, either mating imagery or egg imagery which is the result of mating. Ultimately, all our conscious efforts to understand the physical world and reach out to understand the world beyond the physical, we have nothing more substantial than a metaphysical mating imagery of the infinite, determined in concrete verbal or visual structure to remind us of the creative process we are capable of entering into in our physical being under the overriding emotion of Love. Ordinarily we conceive, approximate, mythify divinity in terms of imagery of our experience in terms of political institutions, such as King or Emperor; military institutions such as Captain or Commander; pastoral institutions such as cowherd or shepherd; domestic institutions such as father or grandfather as tribal chief; mystics assure us unequivocally the universal imagery of Lover and the Beloved is germane for establishing prayerful relations with the divine, and such an imagery could catapult us from physical excitement to spiritual ecstasy. Seers and visionaries like Chuang Tzu and his kind in China, Shantideva and the Theras of Buddhist Sangha, Mirabai and Bhaktas in India, Jalaluddin Rumi and the Sufis in Persia, Rabbi Akiba and his fraternity in Palestine, or St. Francis of Assisi, Juan de la Cruz, and St. Theresa in the Mediterranean – all seem to be saying that they have been madly in love with the greatest lover of the universe. Should we then be ashamed of the act of creation or recreation because of the latterday prudery forbidding us from entering the state of Eros, transcending into the state of Agape, and into Philos, where logic is not needed, adornment is hindrance, speech is disturbance, where the will of the beloved yields to the will of the lover and is willing to whisper; "Let thy will be done!" Poetry in its highest vibrations is the whisperings of love, and we have the profoundest of whisperings of Love in the two mystical poems, the *Gīta Govinda* and the *Song of Solomon*, both of which need no defence or apology.

Since the *Gīta Govinda* and the *Song of Solomon* in their antecedental gestation period, and by their impact in subsequent ages, have stimulated artistic expressions in every age in a variety of modes, including music, dance, drama, painting, sculpture and architecture such as Khajuraho Temples, we may find some reassurance in the visual presentation of some aspects of the Lover-Beloved imagery. In spite of the climatic, regional and cultural differences, the essential imagistic framework of lovers provides in every media a situation for expression one of the deepest and profoundest human emotions, Love. The illustrations may help us to see the same thing differently and conclude that the different expressions ultimately mean the same thing : When I am I, and you are you, we are two; when you are me, and I am you, we are one : or *tat tvam asi.*

NOTES AND REFERENCES

1. The title of the Song has been variously used : In Vulgate Latin of St. Jerome c.A.D. 400. *Canticum Canticorum :* in Authorized King James version 1611, *Song of Songs, which is Solomon's;* in Oxford Annotated Bible, *Song of Songs, that is Solomon's.*
2. Edwin Arnold : "Although much has had to be modified, and the last canto omitted, in order to comply with the canons of Western propriety, in English dress cannot-alas-fail to destroy something of the Asiatic grace of Radha; but in her own she is radiant, fascinating, and angelic." — Preface to *The Indian Song of Songs (Gīta Govinda).* Trubner's Oriental Series, London, 1875; reprint : Jaico Publishing, Bombay, 1949, p. 156.
3. *New Oxford Annotated Bible with Apocrypa.* Expanded Edition. An Ecumenical Study Bible. Revised Standard Version. Oxford University Press, 1973. 77 ed. Herbert G. May and Bruce M. Metzger; Introduction to the *Song of Solomon,* p. 815.
4. Rabbi Robert Gordis, *The Song of Songs,* New York. Jewish Theological Semminary of America, 1971 (5721), p. 1 : "The entire universe is not as worthy as the day on which the *Song of Songs* was given to Israel, for all the writings are holy, but the *Song of Songs* are the Holy of Holies." — Rabbi Akiba.
5. Northrop Frye : "The creativity as a feature of human life is in fact what is really a part of our cultural genetic code" of divine creation. *Creation and Recreation,* University Press, Toronto, 1980, p. 4.
6. S. T. Coleridge : 'On the Principle of Genial Criticism' in *Criticism : Major Texts,* ed. W. J. Bate, New York : Harcount Brance, 1970, p. 370.
7. *Rig Veda,* Book X, Hymn 90 : 6-16.

Section C
Philosophy and Speculations

7

From Ṛta to Dharma

JOHN M. KOLLER

I. Introduction

In this paper I explore a fundamental tension in Indian thought, the tension between action and knowledge. This tension is rooted in two fundamentally different worldviews. The earlier worldview, the Vedic, sees reality holistically, in terms of unified process, envisioning the self in terms of agency. The later view, dating from the Upaniṣads, sees reality in terms of permanent, unchanging being, envisioning the ultimate self in terms of knowledge or consciousness. The classical view of *dharma,* the right action that sustains the world and society, although incorporated in the later worldview, is naturally grounded in the Vedic worldview which sees reality in terms of action rather than being. Because the Upaniṣads — and the succeeding tradition — ultimately see change and action to be a kind of illusory covering of unchanging being and knowledge, action comes to be seen as a source of bondage, opposed to knowledge, which alone saves. Thus *dharma,* although enjoined as the right action necessary to maintain the world, comes to be seen only as propadeutic to knowledge, not the way of ultimate fulfilment.

II. Expressions of Tension

The deep tension between the way of action, characteristic of the Vedic worldview, and the way of knowledge, characteristic of the Upaniṣads, is clearly expressed Śaṅkara. In his summary of the teachings of the Upaniṣads, the *Upadeśasāhasrī,* Śaṅkara rejects the view that the self is of the nature of action, announcing that this erroneous view of the self must be rejected in favor of the view that the self is of the nature of knowledge. Only knowledge is beyond change and therefore free from the samsāric cycle. Śaṅkara is explicit : "Actions," he says, "produce association with a body. When there is association with a body, pleasant and unpleasant things are inevitable. From these result attachment and aversion, and from them further actions."[1] These actions are then described as leading to certain results, good or bad, which lead to further identification with the body and further action. As this is repeated, "this transmigratory existence *(Saṃsāra)* rolls onward powerfully forever like a wheel."[2] Because ignorance (mistaken identity of self as an agent) is the root cause of samsāric existence, "Only knowledge can destroy ignorance; action, being incompatible, cannot."[3]

Emphasizing this difference in worldview further, he goes on to say, "In fact, action, since it is connected with wrong conception [of the self], is incompatible with knowledge. Knowledge is declared here [in the Upaniṣads] to be the view that the self [ātman] is changeless. [Thinking] "I am agent, this is mine," action arises. "Knowledge depends upon the real; Vedic injunction [to action] depends upon an agent."[4]

But to think that the self is an agent is clearly a mistake : "That *ātman* is an agent is false, due to the belief that the body is *ātman*. The belief, "I do not do anything," is true and arises from the right means of knowledge."[5]

Śaṅkara's claim that taking the self to be ultimately an agent identifies it with the body, and that this identification leads to actions perpetuating the samsāric cycle, reflects an understanding of action as bondage that has dominated Indian thought for more than two thousand years. This view insists that actions cannot save; that they only lead to further bondage. Liberation requires the attainment of spiritual insight and the *cessation* of all actions.

This conviction, shared by all the philosophical systems except Mīmāṃsā and Cārvāka, is seen in its most dramatic form in the Jaina insistence that to achieve *kaivalya* a person must eventually cease all actions whatever, even those of eating and breathing. The holy death fast while in meditation *(sallehkanā)* is prescribed for all Jainas as a necessary condition of liberation, to be practiced by every person who has achieved the purity and spiritual insight required to enter into this final spiritual practice.

The reason for insisting on the renunciation of action is that every action carries its energies forward into the future making it impossible to free oneself from *saṃsāra* through any kind of action. As Śaṅkara observed, action can only produce further bondage. The whole process of action can be stopped only by the renunciation of action and the awakening of knowledge.

By the time of the *Bhagavad Gītā* the identity of Self with knowledge, and of knowledge with being, had become so well established that the central problem of this text is that of making room for action in an overall scheme of salvation in such a way that it would not conflict with the way of knowledge. And although in the *Gītā* Kṛṣṇa speaks approvingly of action, insisting that Arjuna act to fulfil his *dharma,* he carefully points out that it can be efficacious for liberation only when performed disinterestedly. He resolves Arjuna's dilemma over how he can act to fulfil his duty while following the way of knowledge by outlining a path of "actionless action." This shows how radically Indian views of self and reality had shifted, for in the Ṛg Veda disinterested performance of action would have been a mockery. There is knowing self has not been divorced from the acting self, but is an integral dimension of the acting self. Action, informed by knowledge, saves, according to the Ṛg Veda. Only the later tradition sees action as a source of bondage.

Further evidence of a radical shift in worldview comes from the re-interpretation of the famous parable of the two birds in the tree, one eating the sweet fig while the other looks on.[6] In the Ṛg Veda, it is clear that the one who reaches and eats the sweet fig at the very top of the tree is superior. Yet in the Upaniṣads — and the entire subsequent tradition — the bird who merely watches is regarded as superior because beating is action and is therefore inferior to merely watching, which is knowledge.

III. ṚTA

According to the Vedic vision, however, the deepest and most pervasive problems of life were to be dealt with by finding appropriate modes of action that would embody *ṛta*. Only appropriate actions could heal the most serious afflictions of human beings and provide for a full and perfect existence. The Vedic seers did not regard this world and this life as a realm of inescapable suffering, to be rejected, in the last analysis, in favor of a transcendent realm of perfect freedom.

In the Vedic view, *this* life and *this* world are sacred and worthy of celebration; they are adequate as a basis for a complete and full life. This is attested to by the sense of joy and celebration attending the whole of the Ṛg Veda. It is true that prayer and petition for refuge, safety, and protection are an integral part of the liturgy of the Vedic texts. But this is never in the sense of escape to a transcendent realm of refuge. Rather, it is a seeking of refuge and protection within this life and within this world. Life in this world, lived well and fully, is a wonderful thing, something the Vedic people rejoiced in and celebrated. Indeed, as I have pointed out elsewhere,[7] *yajña*, the most important sacred action of the Vedic age is essentially a celebrative ritual.

To understand the worldview grounding the dharmic understanding of action we must explore the Vedic vision of ordered wholeness implicit in *yajña*, for *dharma* is rooted in this vision. The Vedic view of *yajña* as the effective action whereby the energies and powers of existence are continuously renewed is supported by a vision of a deep wholeness in which all processes and things participate according to an inherent norm known as *ṛta*. Usually regarded as a deep and wonderful mystery *(guhā hitam)*, beyond the reaches of ordinary intelligence *(accintam brahma)*, this vision of wholeness underlies the Vedic tendency to indentify various deities with each other and to go beyond them to an impersonal creative energy that in later portions of the Ṛg Veda is called Brahman or simply "That One" *(tad ekam)*.

But even early verses express this sense of wholeness. For example, one *ṛṣi* says, "I recognize from afar the Ancient and Immemorial One. From Him, the Great Procreator, the Father, are we descended. The Gods, in their own great realm, honor him."[8]

Another *ṛṣi* explicitly affirms that the wholeness of existence is contained in *ṛta*, the normative functioning of reality, declaring, "In *ṛta* I have discovered the wonderful face of the Great One who from the beginning accompanied the Cow of Dawn. It is shining there, hidden in its rapid flow."[9]

In 10.88.18, the poet asks four questions : How many are the Agnis ? How many are the suns ? How many are the dawns ? And how many, really, are the waters (creative sources) ? The poet of 8.52.2 declares, apparently in answer to these questions, "One only is Agni, though kindled many times. One only is the sun, though it rises for all. One only is dawn, though she illumines all this. One indeed is This, which produced all."

In 1.164.46, Dīrghatamas observes, "That which is one the *ṛṣis* call by many names, as they speak of Indra, Yama, Mātariśvan." This is similar to the statement in 10.114.5, where the poet notes that "With their words the wise poets shape the One in many ways."

It is for vision of this wholeness that consciousness must be transformed by the hymns, contemplation, soma, and ritual action making up *yajña*. Agni, divine illuminator of all persons (Agnivaiśvānara), is petitioned to illumine this divine secret hidden in the depths of one's own being, to reveal this wonderful reality that the *ṛṣi* Vena sees "hidden in the cave," the reality "in which all may find one single home."

It would be a serious mistake to think that the Vedic vision of wholeness constitutes a separate reality. *Yajña* assumes that ordinary reality embodies, in some mysterious way, the most profound level of reality. Indeed, it is this conviction that gave the Vedic people their sense of the profundity and sacredness of everyday reality. Furthermore, this vision of participation of ordinary existence in the wholeness that lies at the very heart of reality revealed the normative functioning and ordering of existence, regulating and directing its movement.

This normative ordering, *ṛta*, is the key to efficacy of *yajña*, for *yajña* is the ritual embodiment of *ṛta*, the original rhythm of existence by which the manifest world emerges from the primordial ground of existence and is established in orderliness. There is no exact English equivalent for *ṛta;* it combines aspects of our ideas of rhythm, norm, order, energy, and the well-formed. It is regarded as guiding all forms of existence, giving them energy and existence. According to the Ṛg Veda, the rhythm of day and night, the succession of the seasons, and the cycles of birth, growth, decay and regeneration all proceed from *ṛta.* By it rains fall, winds blow, plants grow and animals reproduce. From her ("the lovely *Ṛta*"), as the dynamic principle of all movement and change, flow the various rhythms of existence. It is *ṛta* that directs the emergence, dissolution and re-emergence of existence at the cosmic level and that gives to each thing and event its own structure and nature. *Ṛta* is both the basic ordering principle of the universe and the ground of whatever is well ordered. Without it there would be only chaos instead of existence. From a social perspective there would be immorality and disorder instead of human community without *ṛta.* It is, in brief, the structuring movement of the underlying wholeness of reality.

Ṛta is regarded as fully present and operative at the deepest levels of reality, but only partially present and operative at the shallower and manifest levels. As indicated in the hymns to the cosmic Person[10] and to the Goddess of speech-consciousness,[11] reality is seen as divided into different portions or levels. The deepest level, the "three-fourths," is hidden or unmanifested. The manifested level, the portion that can be experienced and described in ordinary ways, is only a small fraction — "one-fourth" — of reality. This vision of a deeper reality permeates the Vedic view of existence. "This world" *(aihika)* is frequently contrasted with "that world" *(amuṣmika),* with the latter regarded a the source, and the deeper reality of the former. Things and events in this ordinary empirical world exist and function only to the extent that they embody *ṛta*. And precisely to that extent do they possess reality or being *(sat)*. What belongs to "this world" embodies *ṛta* only partially; "that world" possesses it fully. Since ultimately *ṛta* provides the basis for the being and function of all existence, "this world" can continue to exist only to the extent that it is supported by *ṛta* — which functions fully only at the deeper level of unmanifested reality. That is why all beings must act in accord with *ṛta;* their very being depends on it.

IV. Dharma

Historically, however, the understanding of action embodied within the Vedic vision entered into an uneasy compromise with the *saṃsāric* understanding presupposed by the way of knowledge. The result is the traditional emphasis of *dharma* — which presupposes the ultimacy of action — while at the same time accepting *mokṣa* as the highest aim in life. This despite the fact that *kokṣa* presupposes the self to be ultimately of the nature of knowledge rather than an agent. Sometimes, as in the *Gītā* or in the thought of Dayānanda Sarasvatī, this tension surfaces as an explicit conflict, but usually it operates on a deeper level.

To understand this tension we need to explore the traditional understanding of *dharma*. *Dharma*, referring to right action in the broadest sense of that term, is derived from the verbal root *dhṛ*, which means "to support, sustain, hold together." In its deepest sense it is what sustains and holds together the universe itself. Here its connection to the Vedic idea of *ṛta* — to which it is the historical successor — is clear, for *ṛta* is the fundamental structuring of existence which gives to processes and things the principles by which they act and interact in such a way as to constitute an interrelated whole, a universe.

With the development of the way of knowledge witnessed by the Upaniṣads however, the identity of knowing and acting presupposed by *yajña* was lost, undermining the place of ritual action within Indian culture. As we have noted, reality, according to the Vedic vision, is characterized at its deepest level by activity or agency that is essentially normative, possessing an inherent ordering *(ṛta)* inseparable from its very being. Within this vision, the highest aim in life is to bring the whole of one's existence into accord with this normative rhythm *(ṛta)* through appropriate action, the most effective form of which is the ritual action of *yajña*. The distinction between *saṃsāra,* the sphere of *karma and nirvāṇa* or *mokṣa,* the sphere of freedom, is not to be found in the Ṛg Veda. There action has not yet been conceived as the source of bondage.

But when knowing and acting were divorced from each other, with action seen as the cause of bondage (due to ingnorance), and knowledge the means of liberation, the tradition had to find a new basis for moral and social action. Ritual action, which grounded moral, social and political action for the Vedic people, was now displaced from the epistemological and social centre of life. The codification of *dharma* in the *Dharma Sūtras and Śāstras* may well be the result of a valiant effort to preserve the principles of Vedic social life in the face of threats from the way of knowledge being advocated with great success by many teachers twenty-five hundred years ago. The great emphasis on *dharma* at this time is probably an attempt to secure the foundations of society against the threat of disintegration implicit in the way of knowledge.

That advocates of the way of knowledge should themselves place great emphasis of *dharma* makes sense, for they must have been acutely aware both of the need for society and the lack of support for social action provided by the ascetic, yogic and meditative dimensions of their way of liberation. Thus, it is no surprise that Jainas and Buddhists should insist on extremely high moral standards, and, indeed, make major contributions to moral thought. Precisely because they were *not* heirs to the Vedic tradition which made action central to salvation, they found it necessary to work out views of moral action that would support their views of knowledge as the ultimate means of liberation.

It is important to realize that the Vedic view of ritual action is inherently social. The rituals are essentially public acts, bringing people together for common purposes, providing rationale for various social practices and institutions. Rules of action evolve naturally to protect the social structure which supports the ritual system. Action, of course, creates relationships among the actors and is therefore innately social in a way that knowledge is not.

Knowledge, on the other hand, was seen as essentially independent of action. Indeed, it was typically seen as requiring withdrawal from society because society embodies the world of action. Recluses, ascetics, yogins, etc., constitute an implicit threat to society. Unless the asocial attitude reflected in their practice is counteracted by an explicit and vigorous emphasis on action supportive of society, even if viewed only as a preparatory stage, the whole social structure which supports the way of knowledge is threatened with disintegration. The emphasis on *dharma*, therefore, compensates for the inherently asocial character of the way of knowledge — even as it perpetuates the normative character of the way of action embodied in the Vedic worldview. But incorporated into the way of knowledge, set in opposition to *mokṣa, dharma* perpetuates only one dimension of the Vedic worldview, endowing the Hindu tradition with a deep — and creative — tension.

NOTES AND REFERENCES

1. *Upadeśasāhasrī*, I. 1. 4.
2. *Ibid.*, I. 1. 4.
3. *Ibid.*, I. 1. 6.
4. *Ibid.*, I. 1. 12 -13.
5. *Ibid.*, I. 12. 16.
6. Ṛg Veda, 1. 164. 20-23.
7. *The Indian Way*, John M. Koller (New York : Macmillan Publishing Co., 1982), Chs. 2 and 3.
8. Ṛg Veda, 3. 54. 9.
9. *Ibid.*, 4. 5. 9.
10. *Ibid.*, 10. 90.
11. *Ibid.*, 10. 125.

[illegible]

[illegible]

[illegible] the whole, [illegible] qualities which [illegible] way of knowledge is concerned with contemplation. The [illegible] compensation for the inherently partial [illegible] of knowledge — [illegible] the [illegible] of the way of action embodied in the Vedic [illegible]

[illegible]

[illegible]

8

The Great Rituals — were they really meaningless?

HARTMUT SCHARFE

The strength of the Indian traditions has impressed and astonished Western observers the more they got to know about them. This strength is nowhere more astounding than in the preservation of the Vedic texts and traditions. Extensive texts have been preserved for 3000 years in an unbroken chain of oral tradition, and the corresponding forms of worship are not only remembered but also observed. The persistence of the great *śrauta* rituals of public worship is however somewhat tenuous. They are performed only rarely nowadays, and the performances appear at times more as a learned revival. It proves often difficult for the organizers to find a sufficient number of knowledgeable sacrificial priests of the same *śākhā* to carry out the duties around the altar. Even if such people can be found, their learning sometimes turns out to be spotty. At a *yajña* in Poona some years ago, the wife of the patron *(yajamāna)* unexpectedly entered into her menses, and the sacrifice was interrupted for a day or two, while the priests tried to figure out a way to handle this emergency.[1] Such an interruption is a violation of all rules, and it was caused by the priests' ignorance of the *prāyaścitta* or atonement rites which the Vedic manuals provide for such occasions.

In 1975 an elaborate twelve day celebration of *agni-cayana* was performed by Nambudiri brahmins in a Kerala village. It was recorded on film by Robert Gardner and Frits Staal and published as a 45 minute documentary under the title "Altar of fire."[2]

In two recent publications Frits Staal[3] has raised the question what meaning such rituals have. When one asks modern performers, the most persistent answer is that it is their tradition and their duty; following one's duty is bound to do some good. While they perform the ritual, the officials are totally absorbed in strict obeisance of the rules, and they take pleasure in their precision. Meaning is not on their minds. This attitude reminds me of a Swiss I knew, the manager of a paper mill in Kerala, who regularly attended the meetings of his masonic lodge, because he enjoyed the precise performance of the masonic ritual. He felt in it a pleasant contrast to the cultivated sloppiness of most business activities around him.

If we ask for any deeper meaning of these Vedic rituals, we may receive explanations of single features such as the shape of the fire altar, but no comprehensive explanation, no inner reason for the whole enterprise. Frits Staal suggests that rituals indeed have no meaning. He sees his thesis confirmed by two alleged contradictions in the Indian rituals. Each time the *adhvaryu* (an officiant) puts a log in the sacrificial fire, the *yajamāna* speaks a formula of surrender *(tyāga) : agnaya idam na mama* "This for Agni, not for me"; an offering to god Indra is accompanied by the *tyāga : om idam Indrāya na mama* "Om, this is for Indra, not for me."[4] This formula is followed by the *anumantrana* which asks for worldly benefits. Staal mistakenly assumed that the formula of surrender renounces the fruit of the ritual. It is an anachronism to read the *karma-phala-tyāga* of the Bhagavadgītā, the renouncing of the fruits of action into a Vedic formula. The Gītā, as is well known, demands that one carries out one's duty without attachment to the fruit of one's action.[5] There is no trace of such renouncement in the Vedic ritual.

The Vedic ritual texts distinguish between obligatory *(nitya)* and optional *(kāmya)* rites. Optional rites aim at specific goals such as attainment of heaven or the birth of a son. When the interest in heaven disappeared or when, as Staal claims, the fruit of the ritual is renounced, there would be no point in conducting optional rites — and yet they may be performed as part of one's tradition. This is paradoxical, and indeed paradoxes abound all around us : in nature, in our life, and in our minds. In religion, paradoxes often convey the mysterium of transcendental truths. Still, for the philologist this is a contradiction that calls for an historical explanation. The Vedic ritual of our times is a petrified survival with little capacity for adjustment if any.

When we go back to the first millennium C.E., we find in the older Mīmāṃsā texts a belief in the efficacy of the Vedic rituals in accordance with Vedic sayings like "he who desires cattle shall sacrifice with the Citrā ritual."[6] Great power is supposedly vested in the sacrifice if it is performed correctly, and the gods are secondary in importance to the offerings. A deity is defined as "that which is understood, in a sacrificial injunction, by the fourth-case ending"[7], i.e. that which appears in the dative case. The benefits are derived from the ritual directly, not from any deity to whom the ritual seems to be directed.[8] In fact, it is said that the primary object of performing a sacrifice is not worship or to please a deity. Instead one carries out the ritual because one is ordered to do so in the sacred texts of the Veda.

By the time of Śabarasvāmin (perhaps 5th cent. C.E.) Indra's heaven had lost its appeal even for diehard traditionalists.[9] The ancient descriptions of a life with many women and an abundance of food in a mild climate are now discounted as sayings of mere mortals. Kumārila in the 7th century recognized *mokṣa,* i.e. the cessation of rebirth, as the highest goal. "A person desiring *mokṣa* should avoid the optional rites (which are after all conducted for specific aims), and what is forbidden, and perform only the obligatory *(nitya)* rites and those demanded by certain life situations like birth and death *(naimittika)*. Thus one avoids the sin that would accrue from the failure to perform these two; if one does not desire the rewards of doing *nitya* and *naimittika* acts they will not come to him, as such rewards come [only] to him who seeks them."[10] With that statement Kumārila comes close to the position of the Bhagavadgītā, that praises disinterested carrying out of one's duty.

The primacy of the offering itself over the gods to whom the offering is ostensively made, lets the rituals appear intrinsically meaningless, even though they serve a purpose. We see a change in purpose of these rituals between the Mîmāṃsāsūtra-s and Kumārila, from an earlier belief in the traditional values : heaven, sons and wealth, to the negation of these values and a search for *mokṣa* in accordance with the values of Vedanta philosophy.

We shall descend now into the first millennium B.C.E., the period of the Brāhmana-s, Araṇyaka-s, Upaniṣad-s and Sūtra-s. During this period the Vedic rituals played a central role in public life. Offerings were made to the Vedic gods, and the gods' praise was sung. In return the gods granted the sacrificer's wishes — i.e., if he had conducted the ritual properly. The ritual was certainly not meaningless; but there were deep contradictions. If the gods were not exactly secondary to the offering, they were virtually defenseless against a competent priest; for the granting of wishes was not at the discretion of the worshipped god but followed from a properly conducted sacrifice.[11] The only fear of the sacrificer would be that an omission or mistake in this actions or an interference from outside could ruin the perfection and lead, instead to success, to utter disaster. He tried to guard the sacrifice against such defects through expiatory rites *(prāyaścitta)*. Since it may be difficult to detect all violations, comprehensive expiatory rites are attached to each sacrifice to atone for all mistakes that might have occurred.

Another contradiction lies in the assumption that the gods themselves sacrifice and through sacrifice (to whom is not said!) gain the upper hand in their fight against the *asura-s*. Through their sacrifice the gods attained heaven. This is meaningless, if sacrifice is an offering to the gods, and is understandable only as an anthropomorphic transfer from the human condition : the gods do every thing we do, only they do it better.

If we now regress further beyond the first millennium B.C.E., we find in the poetry of the Ṛgveda truly devotional prayers to the Vedic gods. The gods are implored to a accept the offerings and in return to bestow their blessings. The imagery of this exchange is that of a feast, where the gods are invited to descend from heaven on to the *vedi* and to enjoy the food, *soma*-drink and praise; sometimes it is assumed instead that the smoke of the sacrificial fire carries the offering to heaven for the gods to enjoy. The meaning of the sacrifice is thus much richer. The sacrificer's hospitality is no mere formula, but an attempt, often a desperate attempt, to please a god and to persuade him to accept the offering. There are close parallels to the banquet at a nobleman's court, where the bard sings the host's praise and proclaims the heroic deeds of his guests and is rewarded generously. Strong similarities with offerings described in the Homeric epics suggest that the imagery of a feast was already Indo-European.[12]

But there are signs that even in this period the great rituals were already traditional. The Ṛgvedic poets themselves stress the fact, that in their poetry and in their ritual practice they follow the lead of the ancestors. The gods are credited with inventing sacrifice and taking it for themselves. "The gods worshipped the sacrifice with the sacrifice" said a poet.[13] This shows that even in the times of the Ṛgveda the sacrifice could be seen in isolation from any deity to whom it was offered.

Another indication of incipient rigidity in the period of the Ṛgveda are antiquated terms and ritual acts. The main priest of the Vedic sacrifice was the *hotṛ*. The word is obviously an agent noun derived from the root *hu* "pour" : "the pourer." But the author of Aitareya-brāhmaṇa I 2 voiced his doubts : "Since another pours the libation, then why do they style *hotṛ* him who recites?" Yaska VII 15 therefore derived the word instead from the root *hve* "call" : "the caller" ; but he also quoted a certain Aurṇavābha who maintained correctly that *hotṛ* can only be derived from *hu*. The Vedic *hotṛ*, from the oldest texts of the Ṛgveda onward, does not pour offerings — that duty is left to the *adhvaryu*. The Vedic *hotṛ*, just like the Avestan *Zaotar*, chants. His name, however, indicates that this specialization was secondary. While the *hotṛ* may also have chanted in the past, he was named after his original primary duty, i.e. the pouring of the oblation into the sacrificial fire.

A material reminder of a distant past is e.g. the horse's rib that is used for cutting the grass that will be laid around the altar.[14] Another feature is of greater importance. The Taittirīyasaṃhitā[15] states that the wanderer rules over the settler, and the Śatapatha-brāhmaṇa[16] tells us that the gods moved about on their chariots, while the *asura-s* stayed home in their halls *(śālā)*. The gods won in their competition. The ritualistic sūtra-s contrast the wandering sacrificer *(yāyāvara)* with the sedentary one *(śālīna)*. In all instances, the wanderers get the better of their opponents.[17]

The process of the *śrauta* ritual itself retains traces of the earlier nomadic life style. The sedentary sacrificer has to leave his house and must move about in a highly stylized manner from fire to fire. Though these fires are only yards apart in the classical ritual, a move may take days or even a year, and the sacrificer uses a chariot or carries at least a chariot wheel with him. This is an institutionalized memory of the nomadic past of the Aryan tribes that had settled in northwestern India some time in the middle of the second millennium B.C.E.

Is this now the origin and the "real" meaning of the *śrauta* ritual : nomads offering gifts, with or without animal sacrifices, to their gods, especially the god of fire ? Van Baal[18] has described how an exchange of gifts is often used to establish a partnership bond, the feeling of belonging to a group. The offering should not be viewed as a contract of *do-ut-des* or a bribe.[19] But it is a paltry offering — in Vedic ritual as among the ancient Greek — in which the gods receive mostly worthless parts of the animal, reminiscent of the offerings of primitive hunters : the hunters take the meat and surrender the rest, so that the killed animal can magically be resurrected from the offered bones, tail, ears and head.[20]

We may thus have valuable suggestions why offerings were made — but why were they made in such an elaborate fashion ? What do *śrauta* rituals have in common with domestic *(gṛhya)* rites ? The answer comes from modern psychology and ethology. Contrary to common belief, even modern man is not against ritual per se. He may resent certain rituals which represent beliefs that he rejects, but we can see a human need for rituals. Hippies that settled ten years ago on the coast of Northern California, developed new rituals for their life stages, for their work, and for emotional stability. Old rituals often are imbued with new meaning as society changes. Columbus Day parades, army parades on Moscow's Red Square, and the New Orleans Mardi Gras are modern rituals that dwarf the Vedic *śrauta* rituals. Siegmund Freud used the proverbial couch and transference, modern group therapy gave us the primal scream and aggression rituals.

Nor is ritual limited to man. Modern ethology[21] has found important rituals in virtually all realms of the animal kingdom, especially among insects and birds. They are tied to the basic functions of life : fight for survival, mating and social harmony. What all rituals have in common can be expressed in two words : crisis management. Drought, flood, epidemic and famine are recurrent crises that threaten the whole community just as birth, puberty and death bring about intimidating changes in personal life. Since the presumed cause of these events is often the displeasure or the capricious mood of the gods, it is important to satisfy the gods, preferably before disaster strikes. But the gods are difficult to approach for man who needs a proven traditional framework for his pleas, to overcome his feeling of inadequacy and his fear.

Siegmund Freud[22], the father or modern psychology, pointed out a similarity between neurotic ceremonial and religious rites, viz. "the fear of pangs of conscience after their omission." He also pointed to differences : the compulsory neurosis is individual and private, religious ceremonial communal and public. More strikingly, religious rituals are full of meaning and symbolism, while those of the neurotic seem silly and meaningless. In reality though, Freud noted, even the obsessions of neurotics serve the interests of the individual and have meaning; they protect the individual in what he perceives as a crisis situation. Unfortunately, they hinder his development and prevent the patient from breaking out of his unhappy situation.

If rituals are seen as techniques of crisis management, it is easy to understand the role of the *rites de passage* in human life. Frits Staal had been tentatively willing to concede meaning to the life cycle rites or sacraments. But he noticed their similarity with the *śrauta* rites in which he could not find any meaning. Thus he declared them all meaningless.[23] One should indeed wonder, if nature would have permitted such exuberant growth of something completely devoid of meaning, as according to Staal, rituals are amongst men and animals alike.

There is great anxiety at the birth of a child : will the child be healthy, will it bring pleasure and honour to his family ? Will bride and groom find the happiness that they look for on the day of their marriage ? Will the boy who is initiated to study with a *guru* be up to the task ? Rituals point the participants in the direction that society has sanctioned, and, at their best, they encourage growth. It is a paradox of human nature, that spontaneity is possible in the long run only against the background of ritual. The ritual of language allows poetic expressions and neologisms; but man would risk not being understood, if he spoke only in neologisms.

The *śrauta* ritual was developed and modified over the centuries through the introduction of abbreviated or more elaborate procedures and through substitutions. When the *soma* plant was no longer available, other plants were substituted. With the rise of the *ahiṃsā* notion, animal sacrifices were frequently replaced with vegetarian offerings.

A more substantial transformation came under the impact of *bhakti* and the spread of puranic and tantric mythology and beliefs. For the majority of Indians, *pūjā* (the worship of idols with various acts of hospitality) took the place of the ancient *yajña*. Mīmāṃsā authors nodded their approval, saying that *pūjā* is nothing but *yajña* because it consists likewise of surrendering some object to a deity.[24] The design of the temple with its staff, the sanctum etc., corresponds strikingly to the Vedic altar with its post, *vedi* and so on.[25] The idol of the god in the temple took the place of the sacrificial fire into which the oblations were offered. The vedantic quest for union with *brahman*, the ultimate reality, assigned all traditional forms of worship to a lower level of propaedeutical exercises. All the while, conservative *yajñika-s* continued the tradition of Vedic *yajña*, preserving it in their exclusive circle much like a fossil. The old meanings of the *yajña* are mostly gone now; the question remains, what role the Vedic rituals play in the life of their present day practitioners ? What need do they fill ? And — why are they fading away just now ?

NOTES AND REFERENCES

1. Oral communication by C. Heesterman.
2. Publ. 1976, distr. University of California, Extension Media Center at Berkeley.
3. Numen 26 (1979), pp. 2-22 and in : Sanskrit and Indian Studies (Fs. D. Ingalls), Dordrecht 1980, pp. 119-142.
4. Comm. on Kātyāyana-śrauta-sūtra III 2, 1.
5. BhG. XII 11f. ; XVIII 2 etc.
6. Taittirīya-saṃhitā II 4, 6, 1.
7. Kumārila, Tuptīkā on MS IX 1, 9.
8. Sabarasvāmin on MS VIII 1, 34; cf. P. V. Kane, History of Dharmaśāstra, vol. V, p. 1214.
10. Kumārila, Slokavārttika quoted in P. V. Kane, History of Dharmaśāstra, vol. V, p. 1216 fn. 1972.
11. S. Lévi, La doctrine du sacrifice dans les Brâhmaṇas, Paris 1898.
12. P. Thieme, Zeitschrift der deutschen morgenländischen Gesellschaft (107) (1957), pp. 67-96.
13. Ṛgveda I. 164, 50a.
14. A. Hillebrandt, Das altindische Neu- und Vollmondsopfer, Jena 1879., p.8.
15. V 2, 1, 7.
16. VI 8, 1, 1.
17. C. Heesterman, in : Epiphanie des Heils, ed. G. Oberhammer, Wien 1982, pp. 13-25.
18. Numen 23 (1976), pp. 161-178.
19. The idea of a bargain is not altogether missing in Vedic texts : Atharva-veda III 15, 6 and especially Taittirīya-saṃhitā I 8, 4, 1 "Give thou to me; I shall give to thee; bestow upon me; I shall bestow upon thee; accept my offering; I shall accept thy offering."
20. K. Meuli, in : Phyllobolia (Fs. P. von der Mühll), Basel 1946, pp. 185-288; B. Schlerath, paideuma 7 (1960), p. 307 = (129).

21. I. Eibl-Eibesfeldt, Ethology, the biology of behavior, New York 1970.
22. Collected papers, vol. II, pp. 25-35.
23. Numen 26 (1979), p. 5.
24. P. V. Kane, History of Dharmaśāstra, vol. II, p. 714 fn. 1703.
25. The cultural heritage of India, ed. Haridas Bhattacharyya, 2nd ed., Calcutta 1956, vol. IV, pp. 448 f.

9

Tangible Action: Non-attached Action in the Bhagavad Gīta

DAVID APPELBAUM

The central problem of the *Bhagavad Gīta* is non-attached action.[1] Is there a way to act in the world which allows one to be related to the undestructible, ineffable aspect of human nature ? Ordinarily, one's motives to action stem from the ego which levies the claim of ownership on what is done. "This is mine." "This belongs to me." expresses the attachment to one's deeds which may define an entire life. Although the *Bhagavad Gīta* examines the dire consequences following from a life of attachment, it falls short of a coherent analysis of a way which appears in the gaps of ownership. One must ask at the beginning, what is having ? Studying the entitlements of a material possession like a house — the control I have over it as well as my responsibility toward it — does not fully reveal the internal dynamic configuring the elements of action, inclinations, capabilities, feelings, wants, ideas, memories, choices, objectives, and fears. In this context, the lucid work of Gabriel Marcel, who extensively treats the phenomenology of having, is of great importance.[2] Three aspects of *having* may be distinguished :

(1) My action is *at the disposal of* me in that I have the power to do my will with the things over which I have authority. Having acted implies having been able to act, having the power or force to undertake to act. This empowerment lies at the nexus of claims to the disposability of whatever I do;

(2) My action is something I have essentially *to myself;* it is no one else's. Keeping the act to myself is connected with my authorship of the deed, which I guard by concealment. By concealment, I keep *myself,* the haver, apart from *it,* the act; I stay hidden inside while the action remains outside. This tension of remaining hidden constitutes another part of owning deeds; and

(3) I need to be acknowledged as the haver of my action. Because I keep what I do in concealment, I live writing to disclose myself to the other person as the one who has something. But in the realm of acknowledgement lies the threat of loss; my action can be stolen, misattributed, reversed. So *needful acknowledgement* imperils retaining ownership.

Let *disposability, concealment, and needful acknowledgement* be the salient aspects which make an action belong to me. The *Gītā* furnishes a point of view for acting without actions belonging to me but *acting* nonetheless.[3] To put aside temptations to read a quietism into non-attached action is important. How then are we to approach the *Gītā's* understanding ? I plan to use five clues which the text offers. Building on the analyses contained in these passages, I suggest a way of coming to action without appropriating it as my own. A main support, parenthetically, is Husserl's study of kinaesthesis, the interior perception of body's own movement.

Clue 1. 'Sense-control'. He who draws away the senses from the objects of sense on every side as a tortoise draws in his limbs into the shell — his intelligence is firmly set. (2 : 58)[4]

Interpreters generally agree that an ontological dualism predominates throughout the *Gīta* wherein each and every, phenomenon becomes the manifesting conjunction of the two real constituents of the world, *puruṣa* and *prakṛti*. *Puruṣa* can be understood as the activity which confers recognition while *prakṛti* is the set of conditions governing recognition, or as de Nicholas suggests the 'field of knowledge.'[5] The governing conditions, further, are internal to the activity of recognition and not simply as material conditions. This is made clear at 13 : 5-6 :

> . . . . the (five gross) elements, the sense of I *(ahaṃkāra)*, understanding *(buddhi)*, the unmanifested *(avyakta)*; the ten senses and the one *(manas)* and the five sensory real; desire, aversion, pleasure, pain; the bodily aggregates *(saṃghāta)*, knowledge *(cetas)*, will *(dhṛti)* : this, in brief, is the field with its modifications.

Puruṣa and *prakṛti*, moreover, are not related as mover to moved. *Prakṛti* is ceaselessly active already set in continuous motion by the *guṇas*. In it is contained the realm of cause and effect; it is the cause of effects and the effect of causes. By contrast *puruṣa* enters into an event during a moment of ontological simultaneity — an element irreducible to any governing condition.

> The supreme spirit in this body is also called :
> Witness and Consenter, Sustainer,
> Enjoyer, Great Lord, Supreme Self. (13 : 22)

The activity of *puruṣa*, on the other hand, is through recognition to make concrete the constellation of elements which has the possibility of becoming a situation. Those elements could in some sense enter into a range of other possible situations. By making tangible just these elements in this arrangement, *puruṣa* confers real recognitional contact with what is given. *Puruṣa* is the touch of that which brings tangibility to a presented manifold and conveys it into its actual presence.[6]

The simultaneous play of *puruṣa* and *prakṛti*, in giving rise to all phenomena, devolves in stages through our human reality. Ending with a state of low ontological value, the intermingling then ascends through increasing weight and contact to knowledge and liberation *(mokṣa)*. The *Kaṭha Upaniṣad* outlines the scale of being :

> Higher than the senses are the objects of sense. Higher than the objects of sense is the mind *(manas)*; And higher than the mind is the intellect *(buddhi)*. Higher than the intellect is the Atman.[7]

That which confers ontological weight, concreteness, is the tangible contact with which a given faculty (e.g., *manas*) meets the potentiable situation. Conversely, what contravenes against making real an assemblage of elements is abstractness. Abstractness is abstractedness, the gravitation of a faculty toward interpretative habits governing its use. The stronger the attraction of a representational reference, a symbolic 'counterpart' of the potentiable situation, the less ontological force there is to meet that situation for what it is and render it concrete. The situation thence remains possible but not tangible. It has no life. Thus the degree to which *puruṣa*, through the intermediate faculty, relies on interpretative and representational custom, to that extent is it lost to its role with respect to being, i.e., to remain in touch with the situation. In this case *puruṣa* has lapsed into an unmotivating involvement with the conditions governing its expression, *prakṛti*.

The singularity of the *Gītā's* approach lies in its beginning point. It begins with what in human experience is most deadened, most laden with abstraction, most reactive — sense experience. The narrow range of sense experience expresses passive acquiescence to interpretive habit. Customarily a stimulus attracts the attention away from the situation, forcing one to turn to a representation of the occurrence.[8] The submergence of the attention in the mechanism of response is what Berkeley notes when he makes the *esse* of sense experience its *percipi*. The object of the senses arises with one's reliance on representation; so does the objectifier, the *cogito*. The familiar world of things, standing opposed to 'me', requiring the mediation of my instrumental body in order to be possessed, is here borne into existence. This is the world of *having*. Into this world the *Gītā* injects the clue of 'sense-control.' It recalls us to the fact that where the attention is passively drawn to the impression, the resultant impression seems to be a message from 'without'. The message-theory of sensation, as Marcel calls it, is borne.[9] In its passive mode of operation, the attention, missing contact with the situation, necessarily depends on representations and reconstructions. An active mode, however, is available at the level of sensation. As an experience sensation bears the signature of existence before the internal 'organ' monitoring the process, *indriya* or coenesthesis, as Marcel calls it.[10] Non-objectified sensation, sensation no longer a message deciphered from a distant source, is the language of tangible contact.[11] To this language the clue of 'sense-control' urges that we direct our attention.

> *Clue 2. 'Fruits (phala) of action,'.* To action alone has thou a right and never at all to its fruit; let not the fruits of action be thy motive; neither let there begin thee any attachment to inaction (2 : 27)

Clue I has concretely located the place of non-objectified sensation and has indicated the method of passing from ordinary, habituated avenues of sense-experience to more tangible ones. Control in this context refers to the attention one confers on the incoming impression and has no reference to its content, the given. In actuality de-control is a more descriptive term, since the sedimented habits of perception which 'control' one's contact with the impression are released to a more open, unbounded receptivity. If time were spent exhaustively in inaction, clue I would suffice for disclosing a way toward increasing ontological bearing. Active attention to sensation calls the tangible into existence. At the same time, contact with the one who in reality exists, the I, myself is initiated. In deeper levels of sensation I sense that I am. Clue 2, however, reminds us of the paramount need to go over to action. Transforming stillness into movement does not annihilate sensation nor the trace it leaves of myself. It introduces a new factor, kinaesthesis. Kinaesthesis in a general way is the body's perception of its own movement, internal and external. To encompass action in a search for being, we must develop the *Gītā's* suggestions about Kinaesthesis.

Husserl in the 1920's and 1930's concerned himself with kinaesthesis. In it, he recognizes an intimate relation to power and disposability. He says :

> The 'I can' works directly on or with kinaesthesis, and brings about sensational and hence objective changes only indirectly.[12]

Kinaesthesis is to be distinguished from sensation *(Empfindung)*, which, for Husserl, already bears the shadow of the object.[13] How kinaesthesis further relates to sensation of a non-objectified form remains unclear. Dorion Cairns reports that

> What Husserl means by kinaesthesia is not the bodily sensations accompanying movement or muscular tension, or the inner sensations, but rather something volitional or quasi-volitional that remains when one abstracts from such sensations.[14]

Husserl suggests the kinaesthetic experiences or 'flows' *(Ablaufe)* are the functional correlates of sensations; for example, the sensation arising from my touching the pen is correlated with a complex kinaesthetic pattern potentiating my moving the pen to wirte. Further, while sensation is capable of objectification, kinaesthesis is not. The flows are organized among themselves into fields empowering movement which are coordinated with each sense organ. There is a visual field, an aural field, a tactile field, etc.

The form of the kinaesthetic flow is crucial to discussion. Zaner, amplifying Husserl's thought, suggests an 'if-then' pattern.[15] Regarding my action of writing, the elemental kinaesthesis has the form, *if* the pen is grasped and moved in this manner, *then* a mark is made on the paper. The essence of Husserl's 'I can' resides in an effortful striving to *cause* changes in the object-world or my organism by means of marshalling the potentiating force of a kinaesthetic field. The flow itself is a potential effector, a possible karmic unit. Kinaesthesis provides means of carrying out rudimentary or well-formed desires, urges, impulses, or inclinations which arise successively from the impressions given by the situation. In this guise, kinaesthesis is the empowerment underlying all movement. Its form is that of mechanism: *if* a muscular event occurs, *then* something changes. Bodily experience at this level is highly intricate clockwork but work solely cause and effect.

Returning to the clue about the 'fruits of action', we see that to act in the world is to engage the efficacy of effortful striving at the level of primitive causes. Through kinaesthesis one's body is an instrument of changeful intervention in the world. To act is to activate some potentiating 'if-then' structure, correlated with a sensation. The second observation of this clue reveals that the customary focus in action is not this potency but on that it seeks to accomplish. We repeatedly enact the logical error of affirming the consequent, the truth of the 'then'-clause. We fail to recognize the conditional nature of everything we do. We ignore how the dead derives from a bodily potentiation as integral to the action as attainment. We fail to acknowledge the correlation of the action to our objectified sensations and the sedimented interpretations governing them. Not seeing the matrix from which action arises, we ignore the influence of deep-set habits *(samskāras)* determining our deeds. Ignoring the genesis of action and its determined basis, we are led to presume ourselves the author of our undertakings.

We find ourselves in the position of believing what we does *belong to* us and us alone. Clue 2 points out a fundamental misapprehension with respect to action : that we systematically attribute to the mechanical nature of our strivings the signature of our own identity.[16]

> *Clue 3. 'Sacrifice.'* Save work done as and for a sacrifice, this world is in bondage to work. (3 : 10) Knowledge as a sacrifice is greater than any material sacrifice . . . . . (4 : 33)

Clue 2 described how the Husserlian notion of kinaesthesis underlies all action. It also diagnosed our mortal error with regard to action : not recognizing the antecedent conditions, we identify the result with the action. Furthermore, by not seeing the form of primitive strivings, we mistake mechanism for intention. We regard ourselves as causative agent rather than as the place from which mechanical thrusts issue. Because of this confusion action becomes the problem of disentangling my identity from the engine of the act. What clue 3 gives is the means of extrication.

In the *Gītā's* context, sacrifice is concretely the work by which to approach action. Its meaning derives from the *Agnihotra*, the burnt-offering of the Vedas, in which the object of sacrifice, being combusted, is consumed by the heat and light of the sacrificial fire. When, as clue 3 suggests, the conditions governing one's knowing are brought to sacrifice, meaning is transformed. 'Heat' becomes the friction of the resisting inertia *(tapasyā)*, the momentum of sedimented ways of constructing the object of knowledge. 'Light' becomes the attentive presencing to the ongoing, objectifying experience *(Manaskāra)*. Rather than renunciation, one works towards sacrifice by countering habits of perception and interpretation with an attention illuminating the level of bodily occurrence. The work of sacrifice is, therefore, the work of cumbusting the abstractedness of ordinary experience for the sake of the concretely tangible. Sacrifice is the work of returning the attention to the habitat, the living body, and of participating in its processes whether in stillness or in movement.[17]

Sacrifice is the kindling the flame of the inner *Agnihotra.*[18] Burnt away, the abstractive sheaths cease to intercept the full impression of reality falling on the body's skin which gives contact with the one who is receptivity, I myself. The moment-by-moment sacrifice which invites the return to an unadorned sense of existence speaks in the voice of puruṣa. In the sacrificial moment, the way is cleared for the knower to end his entanglement in the field and to recognize the actional world of which it is co-creator.

> *Clue 4. 'Not-doing'*. The man is united with the Divine and knows the turth thinks, 'I do nothing at all.' (5 : 8)

Mustering the body around its tangible presence, as clue 3 dictates, is the pivotal step toward discovering the *Gītā's* method of non-attached action. At the level of primitive willing — kinaesthesis, we ascribe a partial karmic interpretation to action while ignoring its dharmic context. A two-fold result follows : (a) affirmation of the result of action as primary, and (b) attribution of first-person authorship on the basis of the causal structure of kinaesthesis. Put another way, action is doubly misconceived along the following lines :

(1) In failing to recognize the form of kinaesthesis, I ignore the karmic antecedent to my act. I fail to acknowledge what necessarily *proceeds* and *generates* that part of the action-complex I mistakenly identify as the whole; and

(2) In failing to discern the impersonal nature of the form, I assume the result derives from *my* identity. I fail to notice that in which the causal structure is embedded and from which it actually arises, its dharmic matrix.

Clue 4, however, suggests that the unitary experience provided by returning the attention to the tangible transforms the understanding of action. Recurring to kinaesthesis, one meets the *ablaufe* whose causal from is :

If these muscles A are moved, *then* change B occurs. The flow, moreover, is evident at the moment of the action but anteriorly, ready-to-hand. Already present, the flow persists independently of one's decision or impulse to act on it. Husserl bases his inference on the observation that kinaesthesis is involved in locating a *remembered* actional object, for example, when I remember how it is to swing a baseball bat.[19] Kinaesthesis enjoys a wise field. Memory, deliberation, anticipation, anterior evaluation : the entire actional complex relies on the *Ablaufe*. More importantly kinaesthesis antedates and postdates my doing something in the sense that it is at any time available for potentiation. How does potentiation occur ? Primarily in the matter of selecting some effortful striving for activation, the applying force to form. My participation in the actional complex is like pouring energy into a ready-made outlet. To the extent that I am able to register the experience of a container being filled by a substance distinct from it, to that extent am I able to separate the inpouring movement of *puruṣa* from the receptivity of *prakṛti*.

A closer scrutiny, moreover, discloses not a single Kinaesthes but a constellation :

If these muscles A are moved, then change B occurs.

If these muscles C are moved, then change D occurs.
If these muscles E are moved, then change F occurs.

The embedding matrix of action appears as a set of ready-to-hand *Ablaufen*. The discovery clarifies the nature of selection. If a range of causal leanings is already available, choice is neither of ends nor of means, but of the complex, of a certain karmic tendency. Where one thinks solely in terms of ends and means, a karmic debt is incurred. One remains oblivious to the mechanical connection binding result to antecedent and antecedent to result, thereby running the risk of entanglement in the unsensed clockwork of the act. This matrix furnishes an understanding of the dharma of the act, its context of meaning : for the meaning of any particular kinaesthesis is given only against the background of its competing and alternative flows (the field.')

When my role is selectively to energize causal propensities ready-to-hand, I am less prone to presume myself author of the attainment. Neither the consequent nor the antecedent *belong to* me, nor does the causal connection binding them. The result is not something I 'do'. My part seems rather to consist, in a fashion not fully obvious, in marking that a given kinaesthesis has been *thouched off*. In a way that need not imply haphazardness or random selection, I observe that a specific means-end complex is hit upon whose action changes the face of the world. Nor does it seem that *I* actually touch of a primitive striving. By the fact that effort is applied (in the passive voice), it is more accurate to say that the potentiating force goes with the kinaesthesis in a pre-established harmony. The *Gītā's* action operates in a Leibnizian universe. The conjunction is as close as I am able to come to witnessing the marriage of *puruṣa* and *prakṛti*, the one that motivates and the one that is ready to be moved. Beholding that which occurs, I witness the wedding of the primal forces under the canopy of my flesh.

> *Clue 5. 'Concentration (dhyāna)'* Let the yogin try constantly to concentrate his mind remaining in solitude and alone, self-controlled, free from desires, and longing for possessions. (6.10)

Clues 1 through 4 laid bare the phenomena on which the *Gītā* moves. Clue 5 consolidates a way towards non-attached action. It formulates an ontological approach which allows one to near the mode of non-possessing action. Concentration *(dhyāna)* is the means of returning the attention to the tangible, away from interpretative abstractedness, toward the kinaesthetic matrix. In the language of clue 1, *dhyāna* is the shift in *manas* from a passive to an active mode, from a substantive to a verbial understanding of 'mind'. *Manas* activated operates in harmony with *buddhi,* the intellect.[20] Activated, it is able to touch the lived body in action.

With the structure of kinaesthesis we reconsider the tripartite idea of having. Having, it will be recalled, involves (1) disposability, (2) concealment, and (3) needful acknowledgement. How can I act in such a way that the action does not *belong* to me ? With regard to disposability, the focus of potency shifts from an identity I call myself to the meeting of a potentiating force with a potentiable structure. No longer is it that I stand as the agent empowering the act, but rather as the witness to that joining which is empowerment, of *puruṣa* and *prakṛti*. I am the one who keeping touch with the actional conjugates, allows the birth of the act. Second, with regard to concealment, the action is not an event I can keep secret to myself. While having a genesis within the habitat of my body, the components are not personal nor private. Their existence is both 'within' me and 'without', or neither. The fact that the conjunction of actional components takes place nearer me confers no special privileges, duties, nor responsibilities with respect to it. This troublesome conclusion raises moral difficulties about the *Gītā's* proposals which I will not consider. Finally, regarding my need for acknowledgement, no insurance against the action's being lost to or stolen from me is required. When the act no longer belongs to me, I have gained a freedom relative to its occasion. The freedom allows participation without involvement. I am not remote from the action. I am as near to its source as is possible. Being near, I give witness to tangible evidence that the source is not *in* me. The place given me by the location of my body provides a vehicle for the source of all action. Action in this final stage of recognition becomes an expression of the blending of a bipolar reality. I am the first attendant to the act.

I do not address the objection that the *Gītā's* method distorts the meaning both the action and of myself as agent. The hidden agenda, *mokṣa,* pushes the analysis necessarily beyond the ordinary sense of agency. More important is to ask whether the method encompasses a means of verification, and whether the tangible evidence of sensation and kinaesthesis attests with sufficient strength to an approaching reality.

NOTES AND REFERENCES

1. Minor notes this fact : 'The key to right action, however, as has been noted again and again is that the actions are performed must be performed without concern for the results.' ('The *Gita's* way as the only way,' *Philosophy East & West,* 30, no. 3 (July 1980 : 339-354). Compare : R. K. Garg., 'The Gita-Principle of Detached Activism', *Prabuddha Bharata* 74 (July 1969) : 310-314; J.T.F. Jordens, 'Bhagavadgita : Karma Exorcised', *Millawa-Millu,* the Australian Bulletin of Comparative Religion" (1964) : 22-30; B. Kuppuswamy, 'The Concept of Work According to Gita', *Prabuddha Bharata* 69 (November 1964) : 465-469.
2. See especially, 'Outlines of a Phenomenology of Having,' in *Being and Having,* tr. K. Farrer, (New York, Harper & Row, 1965); and *Metaphysical Journal,* tr. B. Wall. (Chicago, Henry Regnery, 1952). Richard Zaner provides a perspicious summary of Marcel's ideas on having, in *The Problem of Embodiment* (The Hague, Martinus Nighoff, 1971) pp. 21-35.
3. It is important to emphasize that the way to non-attachment through *inaction* is blocked. Cf.
   But do not let yourself by attached to inaction either (2 : 47), and
   For no one can remain absolutely inactive even for a moment. Everyone is made to engage in action, however unwillingly, by way of *guṇas* born of *prakṛti* (3 : 5)
4. I have taken translations from de Nicolás, *Avatara* (New York, Nicolas Hays Ltd., 1976), pp. 79-163.
5. *Op. cit.,* Chapter 5, pp. 189-233.
6. In this sense, *puruṣa* could be compared to the role feeling plays in Whitehead's idea of the emergence of an actual event.
7. 3 : 10 ; cf. 3 : 42.
8. Merleau-Ponty distinguishes between primary and secondary attention so that reactive attraction is contrasted with intentional placements of the attention. Such a distinction derives from Husserl's discussion of

sedimentation of the pre-reflective, non-objectified life-world. See Merleau-Ponty, *Phenomenology of Perception,* tr. C. Smith (New York, Humanities Press, 1962), p. 130.

9. *Metaphysical Journal,* p. 220.
10. *Ibid.*, p. 19.
11. Cf. Erwin Straus' extended discussion of sensing as a mode of perceiving; in *The Primary World of Senses,* tr. Jacob Needleman (New York, Macmillan, 1963), Part IV, pp. 189-396.
12. In Dorian Cairns, *Conversation with Husserl and Fink* (The Hague, Martinus Nijhoff, 1976) p. 4.
13. *Empfinding* consisting of 'reflections and shadows' *(Abschatten)* of objects.
14. *Op. cit.*, p. 64.
15. *The Context of Self* (Athens, Ohio, Ohio University Press, 1981), p. 59.
16. The faculty to which is customarily ascribed the mistaken affirmation of the consequent (and the erroneous basis of personal identity it entails) is the *ahamkara.*
17. It is not identical with renunciation, e.g., 3 : 4.
18. Cf. Coomaraswamy, '*Atmayajna* : Self-Sacrifice', in *Selected Papers 2,* ed. R. Lipsey. (Princeton, Bollinger Sevier LXXXIX, 1977) pp. 107-147.
19. in Cairns, *op. cit.*, p. 5.
20. Cf. *Katha Upanishad* 3. 3-3. 6.

Section D

Arts and Sciences and Medicine In Sanskrit Era

10

Education in the Age of the Upaniṣads

GOPAL C. BHATTACHARYYA

In his book *Ancient Indian Education*, Radha Kumud Mookerji mentions in the very preface :

> "India is still in request in the world for the treasures of her thought. These treasures are embodied in Sanskrit literature . . . . which is remarkable in the literature of the world for its vastness, volume, variety, quality and longevity, and justifies the education of which it is the product."[1]

Richness and variety of Indian culture perhaps justifies an inquiry into the system of education which produced such a culture. Observing the vastness of the literature again and in some disciplines its relevance to modern thoughts, one naturally wonders what sort of upbringing was responsible for such a host of creative talents. A research scholar, it is presumed, would be interested in discovering the sort of education that preserved and transmitted this variegated culture and civilization generation after generation for more than four thousand years, particularly at a time when printing and modern means of communication were not known.[2]

A student of Sanskrit literature comes across a system of education not only during the period of the Ṛg Veda, which is regarded as the earliest record of human thought (1500 BC)[3], but also during the later Vedic period (800-700 BC) and not to speak of still later periods. The aim of this paper, however, is to investigate the literature of the

Upaniṣads, which is regarded as the 'product of the highest wisdom'[4] to find out the educational system during that period.

The Upaniṣads are the closing chapters or the end (anta) of the Vedas. Bādarāyaṇa attempted to systematise the teachings of the Upaniṣads in Sūtras which are known as Brahma Sūtras or Vedānta Sūtras and also known as Śarīraka Sūtras.[5] The era of the Vedānta is regarded as the most creative period of Indian thought. It is a period when there was a remarkable achievement not only in the quest of Reality, but also it was the age when other branches of knowledge were also cultivated.[6]

Upaniṣads come under Arthavāda of the Vedas which include explanations of the practical instructions (Vidhi) for sacrifice later taking the form of philosophical speculation on the nature of Reality. The education coming under the period of the Upaniṣads was based on the Vedic Schools which were the ancient seats of learning and, in fact, were "colonies in which were centered the talent, the piety, the culture of the community, from which they radiated in all directions."[7]

How many Upaniṣads there once were is difficult to ascertain. Of these at present 108 can be traced. Though they differ in "style and manner", their teachings are consistent. Of these 108 again Śaṃkara had recognised 16 as authentic, but he wrote commentaries on 10 only and these are : Īśhā, Kena, Kaṭha, Praśna, Muṇḍaka, Māṇḍūkya, Chāndogya, Bṛhadāraṇyaka, Aiteraya, and Taittirīya.[8] For our study for this paper we will limit ourselves to these ten Upaniṣads and the Śvetāśvatara and the Maitrī Upaniṣads.

The aim of human life according to the teachings of the Vedas including the Upaniṣads is fourfold : Dharma (righteousness), Artha (wealth), Kāma (enjoyment) and Mokṣa or spiritual freedom (liberation).[9] This again is related to four successive stages of life, called Aśramas : Brahmacarya (period of student-life), Gārhasthya (period of life of a householder), Vānaprasthya period of retirement) and Saññyāsa (period of renunciation).[10] The concept and the aims of education of the age of the Upaniṣads were directly related to the aims of life and were concerned with the twofold path, Preyas and Sreyas, i.e., "world-life with the everlasting beyond."[11]

Admission to studentship was inaugurated by Upanayana which means the celebration of bringing the student near the teacher.[12] The teacher would take charge of the student by holding his (latter's) right hand and touching his heart and praying to the Sun that the student's intellect be stimulated and that there is "harmonious co-operation in keen and vigorous studies."[13] In the text of the Taittîya Upanisad (Chapter II) and in the invocation of Kaṭha Upaniṣad we find the prayer of the teacher as follows :

> Saha nāvavatu, saha nau bhunaktu, saha vîryam karavāvahai : tejasvināvadhîtam astu : mā vidviṣāvahai; Auṁ Sántiḥ, Śāntiḥ, Śāntiḥ.

> "May He protect us both; may He be pleased with us both; may we work together with vigor; may our study make us illumined; may there be no dislike between us. Aum, Peace, Peace, Peace."[14]

In some places we find the teacher praying for more students : "As waters run downward, as months into the year, so into me, may students of sacred knowledge come."[15] This desire for more students was not for any worldly benefit, but for propagation of the truths they had discovered.

In the process of gaining knowledge the need of the teacher was held indispensable. In the Kaṭha Upaniṣad we find : "Arise, awake, and approaching the best of Teachers (Saṁkara's interpretation) know (the world of Reality.)"[16] In the Chāndogya Upaniṣad a teacher is regarded as a person who removes the bandage of a blindfolded man who wants to find his way home.[17]

In such a scheme of education it is just natural that the teacher was expected to possess all that is best in human beings. Kaṭha Upaniṣad says:

na nareṇāvareṇa prokta eṣa suvijñeyo bahudhā cintyamānaḥ (I. 2.8).

"Taught by an inferior man He cannot be truely understood as He is thought of in many ways."[18]

The Muṇḍaka Upaniṣad says :

"Tad vijñānārthaṁ sa gurum evābhigacchet samit-pāṇiḥ śrotriyam brahma-niṣṭham." (I. 2.12).

"For the sake of this knowledge, let him (a student) only approach, with a sacrificial fuel in hand, (that means for admission) a teacher who is learned in the scriptures and established in Brahman."[19]

In Praśna Upaniṣad the teacher says:

nāham imaṁ veda, ydyaham imam avediṣaṁ kathaṁ te nāvakṣyam iti, samūlo vā eṣa pariśuṣyati yo'nṛtam abhivadati, tasmām nārhāmy anṛtaṁ vaktum . . . . . (VI. I)

"I know him (the person with sixteen parts) not. If I had known him, why should I not tell you about it. Verily, to his roots, he withers, who speaks untruth. Therefore, it is not proper for me to speak untruth."[20]

It was the duty of the teacher to teach his student exactly as he would know. Mundaka Upanisad advises :

"Unto him who has approached in due form, whose mind is tranquil and who has attained peace, let the knowledgeable (teacher) teach in its very truth that Knowledge about Brahman by which one knows the imperishable person, the true."[21]

Sometimes, as was the case with Śvetaketu Āruṇeya, in Chāndogya Upaniṣad (Chapter VI, Section 1), the father, Sage Uddālaka, would be the teacher. Śvetaketu's father become his teacher, although he (Śvetaketu) was sent to a teacher for his education and he spent twelve years, having studied all the Vedas and other subjects with the teacher, yet he did not know of the ultimate Reality.[22]

The period of studentship normally would not exceed twelve years and it would begin at the age of 12. There were certain special duties for the student, such as, begging gathering fuel for the fires, and tending teacher's cattle. Each of these had its spiritual purposes. Begging, as for example, would produce in the student a spirit of humbleness, tending the fire would enkindle the mind of the student, and tending cattle or guarding the teacher or teacher's house would make the student feel living the life as a member of the teacher's family (gurukul).[23*]

The teacher-taught relationship was very cordial. The student would look upon his teacher as his spiritual father. Each day of study would begin with a prayer which would mean teacher and pupil are united by a common aim of propagating the knowledge and showing its worth in the life we live. In Praśna Upaniṣad we have the students addressing the teacher :

> tvam hi naḥ pitā yo'smākam vidyāyāḥ paraṃ pāraṇ tārayasi, iti. (VI. 8)
>
> "Thou indeed art our father who does take us across to the other shore of ignorance."[24]

The teacher would expect that his pupils would speak the truth, practice virtue, study regularly, should not neglect the duties to the mother, the father, the teacher, the guest, practice charity with faith and modesty, (while back at home after, the period of studies). If there is any doubt regarding conduct in a particular situation, the teacher would expect his pupils to behave as the other brāhmaṇa (scholars) competent to judge. As a matter of fact, the teacher would remind his student of all these at the farewell address to the students. (Taittirīya Upaniṣad I, II.

* A student would be called Brahmacārin and Antevāsin which would mean youn[g] learner or scholar leading a celebate life and living in the family of the teach[er]. The same might be applied to a young female student who would then be calle[d] Brahmacārinī or Antevāsin.

1-6).[25] The Kaṭha Upaniṣad stresses control over mind and over purity (of heart). "Samānakas Sadā Suchiḥ" and to have understanding "vijñānavān" for a student aspiring true knowledge. (I. 3.8) study and teaching would be given special importance along with the pusuit of the right, the true, austerity, self-control, tranquility, consecration of Fires, Sacrifice, Social Duties and continuity of the race. (Taittirīya Upaniṣad I. 9.1)[26] The Upaniṣads would require that the student should be calm (śānta), self-restrained (dānta), self-denying (uprata), patient (titikṣu) and collected (samāhita) for attaining highest knowledge.[27]

Their curriculum during the age of the Upaniṣads cover a wide range. The student would start with phonetics, metrics and elementary grammar and etymology for studying the Vedas properly. (The various subjects developed during this period have been listed in *Ancient Indian Education* by Dr. Radha Kumud Mookerji, 3rd Edition, 1960, pp. 105-112. It is included in Appendix B.)

In the Muṇḍaka Upaniṣad (I. 1. 4-5) "Knowledge (and, therefore, the content or subject of study) has been divided into two kinds : the higher (parā vidyā) and the lower (aparā vidyā). Of these two kinds, the lower is the Ṛg Veda, the Sāma Veda, The Yajur Veda, and the Atharva Veda, Phonetics, Ritual, Grammar, Etymology, Metrics and Astrology. And the higher is that by which the Imperishable is apprehended."[28] In the Īśā Upaniṣad we find the justification of attaining both lower and higher knowledge :

Sambhūtiṁ ca vināśaṁ saha
    yas tad vedobhayaṁ saha
Vināśena mṛtyuṁ tīrtvā
    Sambhūtyā amṛtam aśnute (Verse 14)

"He who understands the manifest and the unmanifest both together, crosses death through the unmanifest and attains life eternal through the manifest."[29]

Thus an ideal scheme of education according to this Upaniṣad should prepare human beings "to lead a life in the manifested world with a spirit of non-attachment, with the mind centered in the unmanifest . . . . remembering that the eternal is the soul of the temporal."[30]

In the Chāndogya Upaniṣad we have the story of Sanat Kumāra instructing Nārada as his student (VII. 1 Paras. 1-5). When Nārada was asked to tell what were the subjects he had already studied, he gave a list which indicates what sort of subjects were taught during that period. The list includes the Ṛg Veda, the Sāma Veda, the Yajur Veda, the Atharva Veda as the fourth, the Legend and Ancient Lore, the Veda of the Vedas (i.e. grammar), Propitiation of the Fathers, the Science of numbers (mathematics), the Science of portents (Augury), the Science of time (Chronology), Logic, Ethics and Politics, the Science of the gods, the Science of Sacred Knowledge, the Science of elemental spirits, the Science of weapons, Astronomy, the Science of serpents and the Fine Arts. Nārada added that he had learned all these but words (Mantravid) only; because he was yet to learn what was Ātman (Atmavid).[31]

The teachings of the Upaniṣads by and large give stress on realisation of Ātman and Brahman as ultimate Reality. This is indeed the highest knowledge according to the teacher of the Upaniṣads. The Bṛhadāraṇyaka Upaniṣad suggests three steps for realization of this highest knowledge.

I. Śravaṇa hearing with faith (śraddhā); this includes; (a) upakarma (admission). (b) abhyāsa (constant practice of what is heard from the teacher), (c) Apūrvatā (understanding the meaning immediately), (d) Phala (comprehension of the effect), (e) Arthavāda (Study of the meaning as they are in the explanatory texts) and (f) Upapatti (arriving at a conclusion).

II. Manana (Reflection).

III. Nididhyāsana (Concentrated Contemplation).[32]

For the direct knowledge of the ultimate Truth Brahman, a pupil would withdraw the senses from the object of senses and concentrate on the inner self which, in reality, is yoga or union with the one in harmony with diversities. In the Kaṭha Upaniṣad (1.3.13) we have :

> "The wise man should restrain speech in mind; the latter he should restrain in the understanding self. The understanding he should restrain in the great self. That he should restrain in the tranquil self."[33]

In the Svetāsvatara (II : paras. 8-13) practice to yoga has been described. In paragraph 9, chapter II it is said :

> "Repressing his breathing here (in the body) let him who has controlled all movements, breathe through his nostrils, with diminished breath; let the wise man restrain his mind vigilantly as (he would) a chariot yoked with vicious horses."[34] Also in the Maitrī Upaniṣad (VI : para 18 and 19) there is a description of the method of yoga.[35]

Thus we see the Upaniṣads are fore-runners of the Yoga Sūtras of Patañjali and using yoga as a method of realising Parā Vidyā which would concern the Intrinsic Truth leading to Ultimate Reality and that would be the ultimate aim of education of ancient India.

The Upaniṣads often show the method of explaining a subject by a series of questions and answers as in later years we find in the teaching of Socrates. The pupils in those days were encouraged to ask questions and the teacher would answer these questions with illustrations and stories. Often they (the students) were asked to experiment with their own experiences before they would reach a conclusion.[36] The use of discussion and debate as a method of study led to the development of Logic or Tarka or Nyāya Sāstra.

The Tapovanas or the Sylvan Forest Schools where such higher thoughts were cultured were actually the homes of the teachers which might be principally regarded as the type of school during the period. The system was known as Gurukul which would actually mean a student receiving education, living the life as a member of the family (kul) of the teacher (Guru).[37]

The Kings of the country would patronage the education of those days by inviting the learned scholars of their times for discussion of the truths of life as known by the scholars. It was in such academic meetings or conferences that the truths of life and metaphysics were thrashed out and the studies of earlier years of the scholars were tested and matured through criticism and analysis.[38]

NOTES AND REFERENCES

1. *Ancient Indian Education* (Brāhminical and Buddhist) by Radha Kumud Mookerji, Motilal Banarsidass, Delhi, Third Edition, 1960, Prologue p. XXXVI.
2. *Education in Ancient India* by A. S. Altekar, Nanda Kisore & Bros., Banasphatak, Varanasi, India, 1965, p. 1.
3. *A Source Book in Indian Philosophy,* Edited by S. Radhakrishnan and Charles A. Moore, Princeton University Press, Princeton, New Jersey, 1973, p. 3.
4. *Ibid.,* p. 37.
5. *Indian Philosophy* by S. Radhakrishnan, Volume II, George Allen Unwin Ltd., New York, The Macmillan Company, 1931, p. 430.
6. *Ancient Indian Education,* Ibid, pp. 84-85 and *Indian Philosophy,* ibid, Volume 1, pp. 137-139.
7. *Ancient Indian Education,* Ibid, p. 85.
8. *The Spiritual Heritage of India* by Swami Prabhavananda, Vedanta Press, Hollywood, California, 1969, p. 40.
9. *Renascent Hinduism* by D. S. Sarma, Bharatiya Vidya Bhavan, Chowpathy, Bombay-7, p. 26. The four aims of life are known as Puruṣārthas.
10. *The Hindu View of Life* by S. Radhakrishnan, London : George Allen & Unwin Ltd., New York : The Macmillan Company, 1941, p. 82 and *The Spiritual Heritage of India,* Ibid, p. 37. Professor Paul Deussen's view is that the division of each of the Vedas into Saṁhitās, Brāhmaṇas, Āraṇyakas and Upaniṣads is based on the principle of dividing life into four successive stages : Student-life, life of a householder, life of retirement and life of renunciation. These stages may be divided according to age as follows : Admission to student life came at the age of 12. The period of student life lasted up to the age of 24. The householder period lasted up to the age of 50. After the age of 50 came the periods of retirement and renunciation (Panchāśūrdhve Vanam Vrajet).
11. *Ancient Indian Education, Ibid.* p. 156.
12. *Education in Ancient India, Ibid,* p. 301. The detailed description of the Upanayana ceremony is given in Appendix A.
13. *The Principal Upaniṣads* by S. Radhakrishnan, Harper and Brothers Publishers, New York, p. 594.
14. *Ibid.,* p. 594. Also *Ibid,* p. 574 : Īśā Upanisad. The verse explains: To understand consciousness of oneness and consciousness of multiplicity which are termed as Vidyā and Avidyā or Sambhūtiṁ or Vināśaṁ as in Verse

14 of the same. Upanisad is the perfect aim or ideal of education and of life. These may be taken as ultimate and proximate aims respectively leading to the Supreme.

15. *Ibid.*, p. 531.
16. *Ibid.*, p. 628.
17. *Ibid.*, p. 464 and *Education in Ancient India*, Ibid, p. 89 notes from the Chāndogya Upanisad (V, 14, 1-2). "Precisely my dear sir, as a man who has been brought blindfolded from the country of Gandhārā and then set at liberty at a place where there are no human beings, and just as that person would shout towards the east or north or south or west, 'I have been brought here blindfolded and blindfolded set at liberty.' And as, (after that) someone has taken off the bandage, and has told him, 'In this direction Gandhārā lies, go in this direction.' 'Thereupon instructed and prudent, asking the road from village to village, he finds his way home to Gandhārā; even so the man who in this world has met with a teacher, becomes conscious. 'To this (transitory world) shall I belong only until the time of my release, thereupon shall I reach perfection."
18. *The Principal Upaniṣads, Ibid*, p. 610.
19. *Ibid.*, pp. 678-79.
20. *Ibid.*, p. 666.
21. *Ibid.*, p. 679.
22. *Ibid.*, p. 446.
23. *Ancient Indian Education, Ibid*, pp. 93-94.
24. *The Principal Upaniṣads, Ibid.*, p. 668.
25. *Ibid.*, pp. 537-39.
    The farewell address to the departing students by the teacher is given in full in Appendix C.
26. *Ibid.*, pp. 536.
27. *Ancient Indian Education, Ibid*, pp. 95-96.
28. *The Principal Upanisads, Ibid*, p. 672.
30. *Ibid*, p. 577.
31. *Ibid.*, pp. 468-70.
32. *Ancient Indian Education, Ibid.*, p. 114.
33. *The Principal Upanisads, Ibid.*, pp. 627-28, especially verse 13.
34. *Ibid.*, p. 721, verses 8 through 13.
35. *Ibid.*, pp. 830-31, verses 18 and 19.
36. *Ancient Indian Education, Ibid.*, pp. 112-13.
37. *Ibid.*, Prologue XXVII.
38. *Ibid.*, p. 135.

11

Lāsya : Dance or Drama ?

MANDAKRANTA BOSE

In the critical literature of the performing arts of classical India, there is some confusion about what is meant by the term lāsya. It is usually regarded today as a feminine, delicate style of dancing distinct from the tāṇḍava style described by Bharata in the *Nāṭyaśāstra*. There is, however, no authority for this view in the *Nāṭyaśāstra* which, on the contrary, compares lāsya with bhāṇa, that is, a form of drama :

अन्यान्यपि लास्यविधावङ्गानि तु नाटकोपयोगिनि ।
अस्माद्विनिःसृतानि तु भाण इवैकप्रयोज्यानि ॥
भाणाकृतिवल्लास्यं विज्ञेयं त्वेकपात्रहार्यं वा ।
प्रकरणवदुह्यं कार्यासंस्तवयुक्तं विविधभावम् ॥

(*NS* 19. 117-118)

> In lāsya there are other features that are suitable for drama. These elements are derived from drama and, like bhāṇa, are to be performed by a single person.
> Lāsya has a form similar to bhāṇa, which has to be performed by a single person. As in prakaraṇa, its action is imagined and expresses a variety of sentiments.

It was only in later works on dance and drama that lāsya came to be firmly identified as a category of dancing and as a vehicle of feminine moods.[1]

The chief reason for associating lāsya with feminine qualities lies in the legends relating to the origins of dance and drama cited by early writers. Bharata identified Tandu as the first exponent — as the direct disciple and servant of Śiva — of the dance, which thereby came to be known by the term tāṇḍava.[2] In similar fashion, Nāndīkeśvara reports in his *Abhinayadarpaṇa* that lāsya was taught by Pārvatī.[3] It is therefore understandable that tāṇḍava and lāsya should have come to be associated, respectively, with masculine and feminine qualities, and with male and female dancers. This segregation never appears in the *Nāṭyaśāstra*.

An interesting point to note is that by Bharata's definition nothing that falls outside the category of tāṇḍava could be called a dance form. The evidence appears clearly in the text :

नृत्तप्रयोगः सृष्टो यः स ताण्डव इति स्मृतः ।

(*NS* 4.261)

What was created as dance is known as tāṇḍava.

We must note that the term used by Bharata for dancing is not nṛtya but nṛtta, which he defines as an art that carries no meaning :

- अत्रोच्यते न खल्वर्थं कंचिन्नृत्तमपेक्षते ।

(*NS* 4.263)

It is said that dance does not require any meaningful content.

In the light of this definition Bharata could not have viewed lāsya as dancing. That he regarded lāsya as a dramatic art is evident from his description of the ten forms of lāsya that he mentions :[4]

आसनेषूपविष्टैर्यत्तन्त्रीभाण्डोपबृंहितम् ।
गायनैर्गायते शुष्कं तद्गेयपदमुच्यते ॥
प्राकृतं यद्वियुक्ता तु पठेदात्तरसं स्थिता ।
मदनानलतप्ताङ्गी स्थितपाठ्यं तदुच्यते ॥
आसीनमास्यते यत्र सर्वातोद्यवर्जितम् ।

अप्रसारितगात्रं च चिन्ताशोकसमन्वितम् ॥
वृत्तानि विविधानि स्युर्गेयं गाने च संश्रितम् ।
चेष्टाभिश्चाश्रयः पुंसां यत्र सा पुष्पगण्डिका ॥
प्रच्छेदकः स विज्ञेयो यत्र चन्द्रातपाहृताः ।
स्त्रियः प्रियेषु सज्जन्ते ह्यपि विप्रियकारिषु ॥
अनिष्ठुरश्लक्ष्णपदं समवृत्तैरलङ्कृतम् ।
नाट्यं पुरुषभावाढ्यं त्रिमूढकमिति स्मृतम् ॥
पात्रं विभ्रष्टसङ्केतं सुव्यक्तकरणान्वितम् ।
प्राकृतैर्वचनयुक्तं विदुः सैन्धवकं बुधाः ॥
मुखप्रतिमुखोपेतं चतुरश्रपदक्रमम् ।
श्लिष्टभावरसोपेतं वैचित्र्यार्थं द्विमूढके ॥
उत्तमोत्तकं विद्यादनेकरससंश्रयम् ।
विचित्रैः श्लोकबन्धैश्च हेलाहावविचित्रितम् ॥
कोपप्रसादजनितं साधिक्षेपपदाश्रयम् ।
उक्तप्रत्युक्तमेवं स्याच्चित्रगीतार्थयोजितम् ॥

(*NS* 19.121-135)

In geyapada the performer sits surrounded by drums and stringed instruments, and sings in an unadorned style.

In shitapāṭhya a woman, separated from her lover is burnt with love. She sits and reads prākṛt withdrawing into herself. Asīna shows a woman who, having cast aside all instruments, sits without performing any action, overcome with sorrow.

In puṣpagaṇḍikā songs are sung in different metres. The (female) performer acts like a man.

Pracchedaka depicts a woman who, although wronged by her lover, feels inspired by the moon to adorn herself for her lover.

Trimūḍhaka is a play (performed by women), set to an even metre and full of manly actions, and is composed of gentle and tender words.

Saindhavaka shows a person, who has failed to keep a tryst, reciting Prākṛt to the accompaniment of karaṇas.

In dvimūḍhaka, part of the exposition and progression of the action is composed (of songs) in the caturarśra rhythm (and are sung) to create sentiments and feelings.

Uttamottaka is composed of many different ślokas that create a variety of sentiments through feminine gestures.
Uktapratyukta is marked by a dialogue arising out of anger as well as pleasure, and contains words of censure. It should also contain a variety of expressive songs.

From these descriptions it seems that lāsya was the representation of brief segments of dramatic action which called for the expression of the softer emotions. The dramatic nature of lāsya is further attested by Bharata's remark in a later chapter that

लसनाल्लास्यमित्युक्तं स्त्रीपुम्भावसमाश्रयम् ।

(*NS* 31. 333)

> Since it is playful (literally, shining) it is named lāsya, which expresses sentiments of both men and women.

If lāsya was originally taken as a form of dramatic representation, when did it begin to be regarded as a dance form ? Among the early texts, *Abhinayadarpaṇa* offers no clear evidence, including lāsya in a brief review of nāṭya, nṛtya, and stating merely that it was an art demonstrated by Pārvatī.[5] The earliest text that unambiguously classifies lāsya as a dance is the *Viṣṇudharmottara Purāṇa*, which calls it a type of nṛtta.[6] Another early text, *Daśarūpaka*, calls lāsya one of the two major classes of dance styles, the other being tāṇḍava.[7] *Mānasollāsa* views lāsya as a dance consisting of aṅgahāras,[8] and *Saṃgītaratnākara* defines it as a delicate dance that stimulates erotic sentiments.[9]

A much fuller discussion appears in *Bhāvaprakāśa*, which defines lāsya as a dance composed of delicate karaṇas and aṅgahāras. According to it, lāsya is of four types, namely, śṛṅkhalā, latā, piṇḍī, and bhedyaka.[10] The text then goes on to enumerate further sub-divisions and to describe the actual movements. However, *Bhāvaprakāśa* also states that lāsya forms part of the presentation of bhāna,[11] thereby placing lāsya again in the context of dramatic representation.

The meaning of lāsya has been further clouded by the use of the term lāsyāṅga in several of the texts that came after the *Nāṭyaśāstra*. The term was never used by Bharata in the N āṭyaśāstra, but Abhinavagupta did so in his commentary on the Nāṭyaśāstra He used the term not to mean a class of movements distinct from lāsya but, understandably, to indicate the different components of lāsya. That the world lāsyāṅga was no more than a derivative of the word lāsya is clear from Abhinavagupta's commentary.[12] It is also worth noting that the *Nāṭakalakṣaṇaratnakośa*, the only work that faithfully follows the *Nāṭyaśāstra* directly rather than Abhinavagupta's commentary in describing the type of lāsya, does not use the term lāsyāṅga.[13]

However, the term found general acceptance among the later authors, most of whom view lāsya and lāsyāṅga as different classes of movements, drawing a distinction that has caused some confusion. The confusion is the worst in *Bhāvaprakāśa*, which reproduces in chapter 8 the same ten movements described in the Nāṭyaśāstra. Later, however, in chapter 10, *Bhāvaprakāśa* divides dancing into tāṇḍava and lāsya, going on to enumerate four types of lāsya, two of which — śṃkhalā and bhedyaka — are divided each into ten lāsyāṅgas, which are the same ten movements previously noted as lāsya in chapter 8.

We have noted before that *Saṅgītaratnākara* defines lāsya a dance that arouses erotic sentiments. It also describes ten forms of dancing, calling them lāsyāṅgas, but not equating them with lāsya :

लास्याङ्गानि दशैतानि देश्यां देशीविदो विदुः ।
कोमलं सविलासं च मधुरं ताललास्ययुक् ॥
नातिद्रुतं नातिमन्दं त्र्यश्रताप्रचुरं तथा ।
पादोरुकटिबाहूनां यौगपद्येन चालनम् ॥
चालिः सा शैघ्र्यसांमुख्यप्राया चालिवडो भवेत् ।
सुकुमारं तीरश्चीनं विलासरसिकं च यत् ॥
युगपत्कटिबाहूनां चालनं सा लढिर्मतः ।
कर्णयोर्हावबहूलं लसल्लीलावतंसयोः ॥
विलम्बेनाविलम्बेन सूकं तल्लयचालनम् ।
विलम्वेनाविलम्बेन कुचयोर्भुजशीर्षयोः ॥
ललितं चालनं तिर्यत्तज्ज्ञाः प्राहुरुरोङ्गणम् ।

धसकः स्यात्सुललितं स्तनाधोनमनं लयात् ॥
सताललितोपेता क्रमात्कायार्धयोर्नतिः ।
धनुर्वदङ्गहारः स्यादिति निःशङ्कभाषितम् ॥
किञ्चित्तिर्यगधो मूर्ध्नो गतिरोयारको मतः ।
स्मितं स्याद्विहसी यस्तु शृङ्गाररसनिर्भरः ॥
अभ्यस्तादन्य एवातिसूक्ष्मप्रत्यग्रभङ्गिभाक् ।
गीतादेरागतः स्थायस्तल्लयात्तन्मनो मतम् ॥

(SR. 7.1207-15)

> According to those knowledgeable in deśī, there are ten deśī lāsyāṅgas, which are delicate, playful and graceful movements. Cāli is the simultaneous movement of the feet, hips, thighs and arms. It should be neither too fast nor too slow, and full of horizontal movements done in tāla.
>
> The same action performed in a quick tempo with straight movements is known as cālibaḍa.
>
> Laḍhi is soft and graceful and contains simultaneous horizontal movements of the hips and arms.
>
> Sūka is a rhythmic movement full of feminine gestures and may be performed either slowly or quickly.
>
> Precious jewels dangle from the performer's ears.
>
> Uroṅgaṇa is known as a graceful and oblique movement, slow or fast, of the shoulders and the breasts.
>
> According to one who is confident (i.e., Sāṁgadeva), aṅgahāra is the gradual bending of the body, slowly and gracefully to tāla, and in the likeness of a bow.
>
> Oyāraka is a slightly oblique and downward movement of the head.
>
> Vihasi is a smile full of the sentiment of love. It has an extremely subtle and novel charm.
>
> Mana is performed with a song set in the sthāya tempo.

It is, however, certain that these, mentioned as deśī forms (popular or regional as opposed to Mārga or refined classical forms), are not the types of lāsya discussed in the *Nāṭyśāstra,* because the *Nāṭyaśāstra* bypasses the whole subject of deśī forms; An important point established by the description of lāsya movements in *Saṅgītaratnākara* is that by the time that work was written, lāsya had definitely come to mean dancing. *Saṅgīta-Dāmodara* describes the ten categories of movements included under lāsya in the *Nāṭyaśāstra*. but calls them lāsyāṅgas.[14] It further states that lāsyāṅgas are forms of nṛtya which, it asserts, is deśī dancing.[15]

On reviewing these texts it seems that from the time of *Bhāvaprakāśa* lāsya and lāsyāṅga begin to be considered as two different types. These later texts also state that lāsyāṅgas form a part of bhāṇa. But this position is not entirely satisfactory. Bharata, as we have seen above, says that lāsya is suitable for dramatic performances. In that connection he refers to bhāha, a type of drama which is performed by only one person. Lāsya is similar to it because this too is done by one person. But mere similarity does not mean that bhāṇa must include any form of lāsya. Bharata never claims anything of the sort when he describes bhāṇa in chapter 19 of the *Nāṭyaśāstra*. Since both lāsya and bhāṇa involve one performer, and since in the *Nāṭyaśāstra* the ślokas about lāsya occur just after the passage on bhāna, some relation between lāsya and bhāṇa may be conjectured. But no relationship is actually established by Bharata. The proximity of the ślokas in the *Nāṭyaśāstra* was probably the reason why later authors were led to think that lāsya or its aṅgas were auxiliary to bhāṇa.

Abhinavagupta, in his commentary on bhāṇa, suggests that bhāṇas are chronicles of prostitutes and men who live by their wits.[16] But the *Nāṭyaśāstra* does not mention any such thing. Later treatises, however, seem to accept Abhinavagupta's view. They may have also tried to connect bhāṇa with lāsyāṅga because a lāsyāṅga, being a delicate movement, might pertain to the arts as they were practised by prostitutes. The *Nāṭakalakṣaṇarathnakośa* does not say that the various forms of lāsya are necessary to bhāṇa, though according to it bhāṇa can also be performed by a woman; when it is so performed, aṅgahāras must be used. In this text, the description of ten lāsyāṅgas follows its accounts of bhāṇa, because a lāsyāṅga, like a bhāna, is performed by a single actor.[17]

The history of lāsya makes the evolution of the performing arts of India particularly interesting. As we have seen in the survey made above, the term lāsya is never used in the *Nāṭyaśāstra* to denote dancing of any kind. Instead, that text accords lāsya the same status as a performing art as it gives bhāṇa. Lāsya and bhāṇa, nevertheless, are not equated in the *Nāṭyaśāstra*. For later authors, by contrast, lāsya is a style of dancing distinguished by its feminine qualities, while tāṇḍava appears in their works as a virile style embodying masculine qualities. This recognition of lāsya as an independent style of dancing and its separation from tāṇḍava is not found in the *Nāṭyaśāstra*. Since it is generally true that all the later works on dance and drama in India have descended from the *Nāṭyaśāstra*, it may be claimed that the correct meaning to be attached to the term lāsya is the one given in the *Nāṭyaśāstra*. The recognition of lāsya as an independent style might, therefore, have come about in the following way : Bharata's description of lāsya movements shows them to be delicate and graceful; elsewhere in the text he mentions that Pārvatī adorned her dance with "sukumāraprayoga," that is, with delicate grace.[18] When *Abhinayadarpaṇa* ascribed lāsya to Pārvatī, it did so, presumably, because of the common quality of delicacy and grace, and thus gave it the status of dance proper, a status not conferred by Bharata himself. The association of erotic sentiments with lāsya may thus be seen as a result of its association with Pārvatī. Because of that association, as well as because of its essentially gentle grace, lāsya was evidently considered to be suitable for female performers. Tāṇḍava, on the other hand, appears from all descriptions to be a strenuous, physically demanding style of dancing. That is why it seemed to call for male performers.

But, again, such a division of labour is not authorized by the *Nāṭyaśāstra*. As a matter of historical interest we may note that whenever Bharata talks about a dancer, he uses the word nartakī, a female dancer.[19] He could, then, hardly exclude female dancers from performing tāṇḍava, the form of dancing on which he focuses his attention. Iconographic support for this may be found in the Cidambaram Temple sculptures depicting the compositions described in the *Nāṭyaśāstra*.[20] Bharata states that uddhata or vigorous, aṅgahāras are suitable for devastuti, or praise-offerings to gods, while lalita, or graceful, aṅgahāras are best suited to the depiction of erotic sentiments.[21] That may have given later authors yet another reason for correlating tāṇḍava and lāsya respectively with men and women. Lāsya, however, does not necessarily involve erotic sentiments and can also be used in devastuti.[22] Abhinavagupta supports this view when he says that lāsya is meant to please the gods or kings.[23] In the context, therefore, of the earliest source of the Indian tradition of the performing arts, it seems likely that any allocation of tāṇḍava and lāsya separately to men and women would be a matter of convenience rather than of principle.

The evidence of the *Nāṭyaśāstra* clarifies the meaning of lāsya in two important ways. First, lāsya — as originally practised — was neither nṛtta, the pure form of dancing, nor was it bhāṇa. Instead, it was an art-form possessing qualities of both and was a wholly independent art bridging dance and drama. Secondly, lāsya was not necessarily an art reserved for female performers, although it was the representation of feminine moods.

NOTES AND REFERENCES

1. See for instance : *Daśarūpaka,* ed., G.C.O. Haas (New York : Columbia U.P., 1812), 1.15; *Saṅgitaratnākara,* ed., P.S.S. Shastri (Madras : Adyar Library, 1953), vol. 4, 7.30; *Sangitaratnākara*, ed., G. Shastri & G. G. Mukhopadhyaya (Calcutta : Sanskrit College, 1960), p. 69.
2. *Nāṭyaśāstra,* ed., R. Kavi, Gaekwad Oriental Series (Baroda : Oriental Institute, 19650, 4.260.
3. *Abhinayadarpaṇa,* ed., M. M. Ghosh (Calcutta : Firma K. L. Mukhopadhyaya, 1957), 4.
4. In his edition of the *NS*, R. Kavi includes two extra lāsyāṅgas on the authority of Abhinavagupta's commentary. In view of Bharata's categorical statement that the number of Lāsyāṅgas is ten, the additions seem to the interpolations taken form some later manuscript.
5. *A Dar* 5.
6. *Viṣṇudharmottara Purāṇa* ed., P. Shah, Gaekwad Oriental Series (Baroda : Oriental Institute, 1958), vol. 3, 20. 2, 4.
7. *DR* 1. 15.
8. *Mānasollāsa,* ed., G. K. Shrigondekar, Gaekwad Oriental Series (Baroda : Oriental Institute, 1967), 16.4.962-63.
9. SR vol. 4, 7.30.

10. *Bhāvaprakāśa*, ed., Y. Y. Swami & K. S. R. Shastri, Gaekwad Oriental Series (Baroda : Oriental Institute, 1968), p. 297.
11. *Ibid.*, p. 246.
12. Abinavagupta's commentary on the *NS* 19. 117-135.
13. *Nāṭakalakṣaṇaratnakosa*, ed., B. Shastri (Varanasi : Chowkhamba, 1972) pp. 270-76.
14. *SDām* p. 73.
15. *Ibid.*
16. Abhinavagupta's commentary, 18. 109-10.
17. *NLRK* p. 270-71.
18. *NS* 4.257.
19. NS 4.278-83.
20. See V. V. Naidu, S. Naidu and V. R. Pantulu, ed., *Tāndavalaksanam* (New Delhi : Munshiram Manoharlal, 1971).
21. *NS* 4. 268-69 and 4.311-12.
22. NS 4.302.
23. Abhinavagupta's commentary, 4.268.

12

Sanskrit Inscriptions: A Quiescent Chapter of Indian Classical Literature

(with reference to Gupta Inscriptions)

MANABENDU BANERJEE

The literary value of the Inscriptions, composed during the rule of the Gupta monarchs (320 A.D. --- 550 A.D.), has not till now been properly assessed. Because of their extensive historical value, their literary merit has altogether been ignored. When we study these historical documents we find, to our astonishment, that some of the inscriptions speak of wide cultivation and sporadic development of *kāvya* literature. Due to high poetic imagination, these inscriptions sometimes are at par with some of the renowned Sanskrit poetic works. Some of the inscriptions may be treated as *Khaṇḍa-kāvyas* in the garb of historical documents.

In order to evaluate the poetic merit of the epigraphical writings, we should bear in mind the purposes for which Inscriptional works were used to be composed. One of the main aims of the Inscriptions was to preach certain religious doctrines and dogmas as in the case of inscriptions of the Maurya Emperor Aśoka. Some were again prepared for the purpose of commemorating the victorious marches and achievements of certain renowned kings. Grants and donations, made strictly for religious or semi-religious purpose by kings and wealthy personalities, were the main theme of some epigraphs. The kings of Ancient India were generally men of letters and they usually patronized poets and scholars : in the sphere of Sanskritic writings. It is, therefore, natural that in the execution of all these deeds, the kings and others sought the help of these men of poetic genius, sometimes the result being that the inscriptions crossed the limits of their purpose and entered into the realm of poetry.

To deal with the history of Sanskrit Inscriptional *kāvyas*, we must start from the Junāgaḍh rock inscription of Mahākṣatrapa Rudradāman, dated 150 A.D.[1] This inscription is incised on the western side of the famous rock, about a mile and a half to the east of the town of Junāgaḍh in Kāthiāwaḍ. This is the first extant Sanskrit inscription prepared in *kāvya* style and bearing a date. It is purely in prose and is the product of the preliminary stage of the Sanskrit prose *kāvyas*. But the language, the style enriched by long compounds, and the diction of this inscription unmistakably point to a developed stage of *kāvya* style. The striking points of this composition are that verbal forms have been rarely used here and that sentences with long compounds run upto a considerable length. It also predicts the future ornate and stylistic prose abounding in big compounds, as noticed in Subandhu's *Vāsavadattā*, Daṇḍin's *Daśakumāracarita* and Bāṇabhaṭṭa's works. A reader will find a fine instance of poetic charm in the picturesque description of the violent storm that demolished the embankment and opened the famous Sudarśana lake down to the bottom of the rivers [*parjanyenaikārṇava-bhūtāyām iva pṛthivyāṁ*, *kṛtāyām*, etc. 1. 5]. Here the language comes very close to that of the *Daśakumāracarita*, though the latter was composed some four or five centuries later.

The Junāgaḍh inscription further shows the beginning of Sanskrit court-poetry which succeeded in getting maturity several centuries later. It also marks the transition period from simple epic style to that of ornate *Kāvya*. In this inscription, though grammatical rules have been generally followed, some irregularities are also detectable. Prākṛt influence on this inscription is prominently visible. Compound forms used here are not, however, complicated and are ordinarily in simple words. Of the *śabdālaṁkāras*, the alliteration stands often with real effect [such as, *abhyastanāmno rudradāmno* — line 4 and *śaktena dāntenācapalenāvismitenāryeṇāhāryeṇa* — line 19]. The author describes the king as well-versed in lexiocography [*śabdārtha*], music [*gāndharva*], logic [*ṇyāya*], etc. (Line 13); he ascribes to the king the authorship of poems composed both in prose and verse, which are distinguished by "a string of epithets as adorned by the qualities of simplicity, clearness, sweetness, variety, beauty and elevation arising from the use of conventional poetic terminology" [*sphuṭa-laghu-madhura-citra-kānta-śabda-samayodārālaṁkṛta-gadya-padya-kāvya-vidhāna-pravīṇena* (line 14). The terms *alaṁkṛta* (line 14), *lakṣaṇa* and *vyañjana* (line 15) undoubtedly point to the author's acquaintance with the science of poetics — elaborate treatises on which appeared several centuries later. This inscription bears the characteristics of the *Vaidarbhī* style as has been explained by Daṇdin in his *Kāvyādarśa* (Ch. I, 41-42). The style and diction, treated in the Junāgaḍh inscription, can safely evince that Sanskrit *Kāvya* style was already highly enriched in the 2nd century A.D.; it greatly influenced later writers of epigraphic works including those of Hariṣeṇa and Vatsabhaṭṭi whose works are no less poetic than those of the celebrated master s of Classical Sanskrit Poetry.

The Gupta period has profusely produced valuable inscriptions, composed wholly or partly in verses, often with certin dates. These inscriptions are studiously written in Sanskrit and there exist at least fifteen inscriptions which are made up of excellent *kāvya* elements; their style resembles that of the compositions of the eminent masters of Indian poetic art. It is not possible to estimate, even briefly, the entire inscriptional literature of the Gupta age within a limited space. So our study will be concentrated mainly on those inscriptions, written during the reign of the Imperial Guptas, which are valuable not only from historical or religious point of view but also from literary standpoint. In fact, in these inscripitons, historical events, religion, socio-political culture and literature have found happy synthesis. Herein lies their distinctiveness in contradistinction to other previous and contemporaneous inscriptions.

The language of the Gupta inscriptions is partly characterised by Prākṛt influences, ungrammatical forms, wrong spellings, indifference to Sandhi rules, doubling of consonants (as in *vikkrama pauttraḥ*, etc.) and such other poculiarities. These irregularities, however, need not be seriously taken note of, for, the inscriptions were intended principally for conveying messages to the general public and they contain words and idioms that were distinguished by the manner people used to talk and also by the system of pronunciation current at that time. Because of these facts, the inscriptions did not follow mechanical line of spelling or other grammatical restrictions. Moreover, several epigraphs were evidently composed by poets attached to the court of kings and, therefore, those sometimes appear to be excellent pieces of polished poetry. But there is no denying the fact that notwithstanding their eloquency and ornamentation, these inscriptions have not universally achieved the designation of true poetry; it must be admitted that since wordly matters and actual happenings were mainly dealt with in these epigraphic writings, there remained, not always, enough scope for poetic excellence. But irrespective of these shortcomings, the inscriptions as a whole constitute an important branch of literature which goes a long way in supplementing our knowledge about Indian poetic cultivation.

The Allahabad stone pillar inscription[2] composed by Hariṣeṇa in praise of Samudragupta, stands out as a distinguishing inscription of the Gupta era. This *praśasti* was engraved on the pillar at Allahabad, sometime probably before 350 A.D.

Hariṣeṇa's penegyric can be distinctly marked as a fine specimen of *kāvya* literature and it gives support to the fact that court-poetry was a subject most assiduously cultivated in the fourth century A.D.[3] This inscription comprises thirty-three lines consisting of eight verses in the beginning, a long prose passage and a concluding verse. The prose portion running from line 17 to 30 forms an enormous sentence, devoted to the description of Samudragupta as a man and a warrior, in which compounds with relative clauses have been beautifully united. Of the eight verses, only Nos. 3 and 4 are fully preserved and other six verses suffer more or less from occasional loss of words. The gifted author claims that this *praśasti* is to be regarded as a *kāvya* [*etacca kāvyam eṣām eva bhaṭṭārakapādānāṁ dāsasya* — line 31].

While the Junāgaḍh inscription of Rudradāman is purely in prose, Hariṣeṇa's work contains both prose and verse and, therefore, it belongs to the type of mixed composition which is usually known as Campū.[4] As it is entirely devoted to the lofty eulogy of king Samudragupta, this inscription may also be designated as *biruda* type of literature.[5] An inscriptional composition has generally some resemblance to the *ākhyāyikā* type of prose works, for, it mainly preserves historical documents. The exploits of Samudragupta are contained in the long prose sentence associated with (many adjectives as well as appositional phrases and a number of relative sentences. This literary device in Hariṣaṇa's inscription was probably the source of inspiration for Bāṇa's *Kādambarī* and *Harṣacarita* which followed the spirit of ornamental and grandiloquent prose-style of Hariṣena.

The present inscription is one of the best examples of artificial poetry, one of the main reasons being the existence of a lot of long compounds in the prose-part. The verses are comparatively free from this technique. Of the *Śabdālaṁkāra*-s, Hariṣeṇa uses only the simplest kind of alliteration, i.e. *varṇānuprāsa* and this occurs principally in the prose-portion [viz., *paraśu-śara-śaṅku-śakti-prāsāsitomara*, line 17; *rāja-grahaṇa-mokṣānugrahajanita*, line 20; *vigrahavato lokānugrahasya* — line 26]. Of the *arthālaṁkara*-s, *rūpaka* is frequently used, and *upamā* and *śleṣa* very rarely. In *bhuvo vāhur ayam ucchritaḥ stambhaḥ* (line 30), the word *ucchrita* qualifies both the arm and the pillar; it appears to be an illustration of śleṣa. Again, in the verse — *pradāna-bhuja-vikrama-praśama-śāstra-vākyodayair uparyupari-sañcayocchritam anekamārgaṁ vaśah / punāti bhuvana-trayaṁ paśupater jaṭāntarguhā-nirodha-parimokṣa-śīghram iva pāṇḍu gāṅgaṁ payaḥ / /* (verse 9), the adjectival phrases — *uparyupari-sañcayocchrita* and *anekamārga* may refer both to the glory *(yaśaḥ)* and to the river Ganges *(gāṅgaṁ payaḥ)*. The phrase — *sādhvasādhūdayapralayahetupuruṣasyācintasya* (line 25) expresses the sense — "of an incomprehensible prince who is the cause of the elevation of the good and of the destruction of the bad (and thus he resembles the unfathomable spirit, Brahman)." According to Bühler, the poetic figure used here is *śleṣamūlaṁ rūpakam*.[6]

Hariṣeṇa does not pay much attention to the use of *alaṁkāra*, but he is interested, as Bühler points out, in the fine execution of the pictures of several situations under description, and in the choice as well as arrangement of words. A.B. Keith considers verse 4 as a rare example of the most perfect effects of Indian miniature word pictures.[7] It describes the time when, in the presence of Samudragupta's rivals at the court, Candragupta-I declares Samudragupta as his successor : *āryo hītyupaguhya bhāvapiśunair utkarṇitai-romabhiḥ sabhyeśūcchvasiteṣu tulyakulajamlānānanodvīkṣitaḥ / sneha -vyākulitena bāṣpaguruṇā tattvekṣiṇā cakṣuṣā yaḥ pitrābhihito nirīkṣya nikhilām pāhy evam urvīmiti / /*. Bühler's remark on this verse is a real appreciation of Hariṣeṇa's poetic capacity. He says — "There is not a word which is unnecessary; and one believes as if he sees the scene with his own eyes, how the old Candragupta, in the presence of his sons, each of whom hoped to have the highest fortune, and of his court household who are afraid lest the choice may fall on an unworthy person, turns round to his favourite son. The verse is one of the best productions the Indians have given us, in the domain of miniature-portraits, which is their forte. This very example would also illustrate Hariṣeṇa's special care for the choice and arrangement of words, a qualification which can be easily seen even in other parts of the composition, both metrical and prose." Hariṣeṇa's *praśasti* rightly deserves this laudation.

The language of the verses is, on the whole simple and avoids compounds of extraordinary length. But in the prose-portion simple and uncompounded words are rare. On one occasion (lines 19-20), a compound word covers about 130 syllables. This type of compound-forms, however, enhances the merit of prose-composition, as Daṇḍin admits that the grandeur of language rests in the frequency of compounds and it is the very life of prose.[8] As the prose delights in the long compounds and the verse eschews them, the style of Hariṣeṇa's 'is markedly and undeniably of the *Vaidarbha* or southern manner'.[9] Daṇḍin further maintains that those who do not belong to the southern school, regard the inclusion of long compounds as one of the main features even in verses[10] This statement of Daṇḍin ensures Hariṣeṇa's adherence to the style of the southerners, the so-called *Vaidarbhī rīti*. It is to be noted in this connection that shorter phrases have also been interspersed in the midst of long compounds (cf. lines 11-12) for the purpose of enabling the reciter 'to draw his breath' and the hearer 'to catch the sense'.

Hariṣeṇa's poetic imagery spreads over the whole *praśasti*. Like a genuine classical poet, he sometimes uses sharp expressions; the poetic niceties in this work justify that Hariṣeṇa's composition came to be prepared at comparatively advanced stage of the Sanskrit literary perfection. This inscription sounds very reasonable when Bühler remarks that "the Sanskrit *kāvya*, which owned its origin to the court-patronage, and which can exist only by means of the same, was assiduously cultivated at the courts'[11]. Metres used in this inscription are *Sragdhara* (verses 3, 5, and 8), *śārdūlavikrīḍita* (verses 4 and 7), *mandākrāntā* (verse 6) and *pṛthvī* (verse 9). Metres of verses 1 and 2 cannot be determined, for, they are greatly damaged.

From the point of view of both style and diction, the Mathurā pillar inscription of Candragupta-II,[12] dated 380 A.D., is much inferior to the Allahabad pillar inscription, though written not much later than the latter. But that the author was not absolutely ignorant of the current literary trend is evidenced by his favouritism to the use of alliteration, as in — *āryyoditāācāryeṇa* (line 8), *Gurvvāyatane guripratimā* (line 10), *parigraha-pāripālyam* (line 14), etc. The language is simple because of the restriction on the compound forms. The last line i.e. *jayati ca bhagavān daṇḍah rudradaṇḍo*, etc. appears to be the half a stanza in the *Aryā* or *Gīti* metre.

The Udayagiri (in Madhya Pradesh) cave inscription of Candragupta II,[13] dated 401 A.D., is small in size, but it contains some elements relating to the author's poetic efficiency. The first verse, though some of its words are lost, appears to be an illustration of good simile. Thus, the available words form the following sentence — *antarjjyotir arkābham urvyāṁ bhāti candraguptākhyam adbhutam.* Here *arka* (sun) and Candragupta have been compared with each other and are connected with the common attribute — *antarjjyoti* which means 'radiant with internal light' in the case of the sun and 'full of internal power' in the case of Candragupta; thus, it is an instance of *śleṣa*. Illustrations of alliteration as well as of the figure of speech, metaphor, are perfectly blended in the expression *vikramāvakrayakrītā* ("bought by the purchase-money of his prowess"). The adjective of Vīrasena, *anvayaprāptasācivya* ("he holds his position acquired by hereditary rights") seems to be an example of *kāvyaliṅga-alaṁkāra.*

So far as various achievements of the kings or their feudatories are some of the principal objects highlighted in the Gupta inscriptions, there are frequent occurrences of the figure of speech, *parikara*, which is defined by Viśvanātha in his *Sāhityadarpana* as — *uktir viśeṣaṇaiḥ sābhiprāyaiḥ parikaro mataḥ.* The present inscription is also replete with the illustrations of this *alaṁkāra.* The language is simple Sanskrit and the compound forms are confined, at best, to three words. The style is *Vaidarbhī.*

The style of the composition of Sāñci inscription of Candragupta II[13] dated 412 A.D., appears to be *Vaidarbhī;* it has no unnecessary lengthy compounds, and short and long words are proportionately used. The adjectives of *āryasaṁghāya* are arranged in such a way that they bring forth effective rhythmic sound, cf. *śilasamādhiprajña-guṇa-bhāvitendriyāya parama-puṇya-kṣetragatāya caturdingabhyāgatāya śramaṇa-puṅgavāvasathāya āryasaṁghāya* [lines (1-2)]. There are some pleasing alliterations, such as, *śrī-candragupta-pādaprasādāpyāita-jīvita-sādhenaḥ* (line 3). Excepting a single instance of metaphor in *vijayaśaspatākaḥ,* there is no remarkable illustration of *arthālaṁkāra.* The inscription has maintained the lucidity of style, as is illustrated in sentences like — *yāvac candrādityau tāvat pañcabhikṣavo bhuṁjatam.* The minor grammatical irregularity like *pañcavimśatiśca dīnārān* in place of *pañcaviṁśatiñca dīnārām* is not to be taken seriously, for, these types of forms repeatedly occur in the inscriptional writtings, probably, in most cases because of the writer's carelessness or of Prākṛt influence.

The verses of the Meharauli (near Delhi) iron pillar inscription of Candra are instances of true ornate poetry and all of them convey wide meaning. They are also fine illustrations of well-known figures of speech. The poet devises the plan to show his skill in examplifying two figures of speech at a time, which was not a very familiar technique with the earlier writers of inscriptions. Thus *atiśayokti* and *rūpaka* are simultaneously naurtured, with their respective grandeur, in the line — *yasyādyapyadhivāsyate jalanidhir vīryānilair dakṣiṇah.* Again, in the second half of verse 2, viz., *śāntasyeva mahāvane hutabhujo yasya pratāpo mahān / nādyāpyutsijati praṇāśitaripor yatnasya śeṣaḥ kṣitim / /* — we can trace a perfect unification of the figures, *upamā* and *atiśayokti.* Here the deceased Candragupta is compared to the burnt-out fire and it is stated that even after his passing away, Chandragupta's prowess leaves not the earth. In the first part of this verse, the expression — *Khinnasyeva visrjya gāṁ narapateḥ* is a good case of *utprekṣā.* the expressions like — *kīrttyā sthitasya kṣitau* glorifying *kīrtti* as the spouse of the king, and — *canadrāhvena samagra-candrasadṛśīṃ vaktraśriyam vibhratā,* bearing the sense that king Candra has a facial charm like the beauty of the full moon, — reveal the poet's mature poetic imagination.

The first two verses of the present inscription express the sense of heroic sentiment. The inscription as a whole is a genuine literary creation and distinctly marks the creative period of Sanskrit ornate poetry. The poet, who probably belonged to the *Vaidarbha* school, is unknown to us like many other inscriptional authors, but he had undoubtedly high poetic prospect.

The Bilsad (in Uttar Pradesh) stone pillar inscription of Kumāragupta I,[14] (date not mentioned), is in prose as far as the end of line 9, and concludes with two verses — one in *sragdharā* and the other in *śārdūlavikrīḍita.* Occasional influence of Prākṛt is detectable, as in *ṣaṇṇavate* (line 6) the correct form of which should be *ṣaṇṇavatitame;* the form — *karma mahat kṛtam* (line 9) contains a wrong Sandhi, the actual form being *kṛtam idam.* Though the style is not marked with any speciality, in some places we find a little poetic relief. Thus, *kauberacchandabimbāṁ sphaṭika-maṇidalābhāsa-gaurāṁ pratolīm* (line 10) appears to be an illustration of simile. In the sentence — *śubhamatis tātaśarmā dhruvo'stu* (line 11), there is a play on the meaning; here the term *dhruva* bears the sense of 'immovable, stable, enduring' and, therefore, the word *śarmā* is *nāmaikadeśa* and stands for the whole name *Dhruvaśarmā*. Or, it may be that the surname *Śarmā* has been placed first and then the real name Dhruva.

The author's fascination for the long metres is, perhaps, for the reason that literature was slowly approaching from the stage of naturality to that of complexity. For the sake of metre, the author sometimes takes the help of tautology as is noticed in the word — *vibhūtisañcayacayaiḥ* (line 13). But this word may have been coined for the poet's fondness of alliteration; to make his prose charming to some extent, he often attempts to display traditional illustrations of alliterations, as in *tejassambhāra samtata* (line 7), *saddharmavartmānuyāyinā* (line 8), etc. On the whole, this inscription demands appreciation not only for valuable information regarding Gupta art and charitable deeds, but also for its poetic merit.

The Gangdhar (in Rajasthan) stone inscription of Viśvavarman,[15] dated 423 A.D. is an important epigraphical piece from literary point of view. It is composed in twenty-five verses. The verses of this inscription are composed in three metres — *vasantatilaka, śārdūlavikrīḍita and mandākrāntā*. Thus, without giving the illustrations of various metres, the author has concentrated his attention to only three principal metres. This was also the general trend of the later poets whose poems included one principal metre in each canto. This inscription is replete with beautiful descriptive verses. In dealing with the characters of Naravarman, Viśvavarman and of Mayūkṣaka, and elegant style marked by the exuberance of craftsmanship is employed. The descriptive passages are occasionally imbued with effective rhetoric. To cite an example, when excellent achievements Naravarman are delineated, it is stated that his enemies in the battle-field field are destroyed by simply seeing his face [*saṅgrāmamūrddhasu mukhaṁ samudīkṣya yasya / nāśaṁ prayāntyarigaṇā bhayanaṣṭeceṣvvḥ / /* verse 4]. This verse is an illustration of *atiśayokti* and the word *khaḍgamarīcimatsu* [adj. of *sangrāmamūrddhasu*] can be easily recognised as a suitable example of metaphor. When Viśvavarman is described as — *aupamyabhūta iva rāmabhagīrathābhyām*. — (verse 5) it seems to be a fine illustration of *upamā* as well as of *utprekṣā*. Again, when we go through the verse — *dhairyeṇa merum abhijātiguṇena vaiṇyam / induṁ prabhāsamudayena balena viṣṇum* — (verse 6), the figure of speech, *ullekha* appears to have been illustrated here. Verse 8, containing the sense that Viśvavarman was shown obeisance by the water lilies in the form of the faces of lovely women of his enemies, who were frightened beforehand at the news of his prowess viz. *yasyārikāmini-(ni ?) — mukhāmburuhair balasya / pūrvaṁ pratāpacakitaḥ kriyate praṇāmaḥ / /*], may be accepted as a fair illustration of the *saṅkarālaṁkāra* comprising *atiśayokti, rūpaka* and *kāvyalṅga.* A qunique poetic imagination is present in a verse which combines in itself both *atiśayokti* and *utprekṣā* in a perfect way; the verse contains the idea that due to Viśvavarman's prominence, the highways are made uneven and at the time of the journeying of his army, the earth, as it were, sinks down under the tread of his soldiers.

— *yasyonnate-praviṣamīkṛkṛta-rājamārgāḥ /*
sainya-prayāna-samaye (bhūḥ) vinimajjatīva / / (verse 10).

In this way the author has sufficiently established his efficiency in utilizing familiar figures of speech.

The poet's expertise in characterisation is best illustrated in the delineation of Mayūrākṣaka who is said to have sprung from a family renowned for wisdom and valour [*prajñāśauryakulodgate*], whose physical strength was reckoned within every region [*diśi diśi prakhyātaīryaḥ*], and who had the self-controlling capacity *(vaśī).* The poet's power of observation is to be noticed in the description of the Viṣṇu temple, of the divine Mothers and of the drinking-well. In these descriptions, the author has left notable marks of his genuine poetic talent.

The author has a tendency towards furnishing, sometimes, the lines of the verses with harmonious ending i.e., ending with the same syllable. For example, *nābhūd adharmanirato vyasanānvito vā / loke kadā ca na janas sukhavarjito vā / /* (verse 13) and *śukle trayodaśadine bhuvi kārttikasya / māsasya sarvajanacittasukha-vahasya / /* (verse 14). This harmony of syllables certainly gives the verses a musical sound and this trend of versification is not very frequent even in the works of the classical poets. It may be safely concluded that this inscription, in relation to the earlier ones, shows a step of advancement as well as betterment in respect of epigraphic *Kāvya* elements.

The Mandasor (in Madhya Pradesh) stone inscription, mentioning Kunmāragupta-I and Bandhuvarman,[16] and bearing two dates (436 A.D. and 473 A.D.), is generally recognised as a noteworthy specimen of highly developed epigraphical poetry. This inscription is composed in forty-four verses and the poet is named Vatsabhaṭṭi. From the perspective of poetic merits, this inscription stands next to the Allahabad pillar inscription. But while the Allahabad inscription is a mixed composition, this one is completely in verse. It is a poetical master-piece, originated in the hand of a humble but gifted local poet who was not a court-poet of any king, but who most probably used to earn fees by writing poetry. Vatsabhaṭṭi says that this isncription is composed by the order of the guild who migrated from the Laṭa country to Daśapura. [*śreṇyādeśena*]. There are innumerable signs of the fact that this work was written with special care *prayatna*]. When compared with earlier inscriptions, it enlightens us about the comparatively developed stage of Sanskrit artificial poetry. The poet shows his proficiency in versification and illustrates twelve popular metres, via., *Śārdūlavikrīḍita, vasantatilaka, āryā, upendravajrā, upajāti, drutavilambita, hāriṇī, indravajrā, mālinī, vaṁśasthavila, mandākrāntā* and *anuṣṭubh*. The poet has often tried to beautify his composition with some essential epic attributes; it includes short descriptions of the cities like Lāṭa and Daśapura, of rivers and mountains, and of the dewy and winter seasons.

The following verses, delineating the personality of king Viśvavarman and of his son Bandhuvarman (who were the feudatory or local kings of Daśapura), are meticulously made to be good poems.

Samānadhīs śukra-bṛahaspatibhyāṁ
lalāmabhūto bhuvi pārthivānām
raṇeṣu yaḥ pārtha-samānakarmmā
babhūva goptā nṛpa-viśvavarmmā / /
dīnānukampana-paraḥ kṛpaṇārtta-vargga-

sandhāprado'dhikadayālur anātha-nāthaḥ /
kalpadrumaḥ praṇayinām abhaya-pradaśca
bhītasya yo janapadasya ca bandhur āsīt / /
tasyātmajaḥ sthairyya-nayopapanno
bandhu-priyo bandhur iva prajānām /
baṁdhvārtti-harttā nṛpa-bandhuvarmmā
diviḍ-dṛpta-pakṣa-kṣapaṇaika-dakṣaḥ / /
kānto yuvā raṇa-paṭur vinayānvitaśca
rājāpi san nupasṛto na madaiḥ smayādyiḥ /
śṛṃgāra-mūrttir abhibhātyanalaṁkṛto'pi
rūpeṇa yaḥ kusuma-cāpa iva dvitīyaḥ / / (verses 24-27)

In these verses, actual but poetic estimation of both father and son has been briefly but efficiently presented. In the description of the city of Daśapura also, the poet has attempted his best to show his poetic skill, but in this respect Vatsabhaṭṭ's composition sometimes appears to be a poor imitation of that of Kālidāsa. Thus the verse -

calat-patākānyabalā-sanāthā-
nyatyartha-śuklānyadhikonnatāni /
taḍillatā-citra-sitābhra-kūṭa-
tulyopamānāni gṛhāṇi yatra / / (verse 10)

— inspires us to assume that Vatsabhaṭṭi has perhaps utilized the stanza of Kālidāsa's *Meghadūta* — *vidyutvantaṁ lalitavanitāḥ sendracāpaṁ sacitrāḥ*, etc. (Uttara Megha, verse-I). When the poet writes — *sumeru-kailāsa- bṛhat-payodharām* (verse 23), he, perhaps, remembers Kālidāsa's idea contained in *stanāviva diśas tasyāḥ śailu malayadardurau* (Raghuvaṃśa 4, 51), Verse 31 of this inscription gives a picture of the season known as *hemanta*. This verse expresses that during this season men are united with their beloved [*rāmā-sanātharacane*]; light rays of the sun and the fire-heat are agreeable [*dara-bhāskarāṁśu-vahni-pratāpasubhage*]; fishes remain down in the water [*jala-līna-mīne*] and people become averse to the enjoyment of moon-beams, flat-roofs, sandal paste, palm-leaf-fans and necklaces [*candrāṁśuharmya-tala-candana-tāla-vṛnta-hāropabhoga-rahite*]. In both words and thoughts, this verse agrees very much with Kālidāsa's verses on winter in the

Ṛtusaṃhāra (5. 2-3). Again, in connection with the description of the *hemanta*, Kālidāsa writes the pleasing verse — *pīnastanoraḥsthalabhāgaśobhāmāsādya*, etc. (Ṛtu. 4.7), Vatsabhaṭṭti reproduces almost the same idea in the verse — *smara-vaśaga-taruṇajana-vallabhāṅganāvipula-kānta-pīnoru- / stana-jaghana-ghanālingana-nirbhartsita-tuhinahimapāte / /* (verse 33). This verse is composed of only one compound word and shows the laboured skill of an artificial poet. This type of composition, which shows more of labour than of poetic skill and which testifies to the poet's love for long compounds in verse, is to be considered as the instance of the *Gauḍī rīti*. This is justified by Vāmana's definition of the *Gauḍī rvîti* in his Kāvyālaṅkārasūtravṛtti (Adhikaraṇa I, Ch. 2) —

samastātyutkaṭapadāṁ ojaḥkāntiguṇānvitām /
gauḍīyām iti gāyanti rītiṁ rītiviśāradāḥ / /

The inscription contains some verses ornamented with alliterations, similes, metaphors and *svabhāvokti*. The lines — *raṇeṣu yaḥ pārthasamānakarmmā / babhūva goptā nṛpaviśvavarmma / /* *(verse 24) — create pleasant sound effect. The expressions like — *te deśapārthivaguṇāpahṛtāḥ* (verse 5), *bhūmeḥ parantilakabhūtam idam (daśapuram)* (verse 6), *gṛhāṇi pūrṇendukarāmalāni* (verse 12), *bandhupriyo bandhur iva prajānām* (verse 26), *rūpeṇa yaḥ kusumcāpa iva dvitvyaḥ* (verse 27), etc. are worthy of drawing appreciation from those who are endued with good taste. Such expressions occur abundantly in the extant Sanskrit *Kāvyas* also.

While Vatsabhaṭṭi has the efficiency in writing charming verses, the harsh sound in the line — *dviḍ-dṛpta-pakṣa-kṣapaṇaika dakṣaḥ* (verse 26) impedes the natural movement of the style. Moreover, there are some other apparently defective features in the poem, such as, the nautology in *tulyopamānānai* (verse 10), needless prefixes in *pra-vijṛmbhita* (verse 15) and *abhivibhāti* (verse 19), unnecessary particles in *tatastu* (verse 22), use of the expression — *nabhaḥ spṛśanniva* (as an adjective of the neuter *gṛham*) (verse 38) and so on. Verses 33 and 39 which are in *āryā* metre, are defective with *yatibhaṅga*.

But irrespective of these minor flaws, we will have to admit that this *praśasti* is a bright star in the galaxy of Sanskrit inscriptions. While the whole inscription is taken into consideration, it is needless to prove that it is a valuable document of wide-spread cultivation of Sanskrit poetry towards the close of the fifth century A.D.

The prose lines of the Bhitari (in Uttar Pradesh) stone pillar inscription of Skandagupta[17] (not dated) containing the genealogical list, have stylistic similarity with those of several other inscriptions, but the verses are the poet's own creation. Metres used for the verses are *puṣpitāgrā, mālinī, śārdūlavikrīḍita* and *anuṣṭubh;* the verses are free from lengthy and complicated words. There are several instances of the poet's fondness of using glaring alliterations, such as — *prathita-pṛthumati-svabhāva-śakteḥ / pṛthu-yaśasaḥ pṛthivī-pateḥ pṛthu-śrīḥ / pitṛ-parigata-pāda-padma-varttī / prathita-yaśāḥ pṛthivīpatiḥ sūto' yam / /* (verse 1); *sucarita-caritānām yena vṛttena vṛttam* (verse 2); *pituḥ puṇyāya puṇyadhīr iti* (verse 12) and so on.

The poet's fascination for metaphor is to be noticed in the expressions like — *kṣiti-tala-śayanīye yena nītā triyāmā* and *kṣitipa-caraṇapīṭhe sthāpito vāmapādaḥ* (verse 4). When in the sentence — *caritam amalakīrtter gīyate yasya śubhram* (verse 5) the poet appropriately attributes *śubhram* to *caritam,* he behaves like an innate poet and, perhaps, remembers the poetic convention which was later on recorded in the *Sāhityadarpana* (VII. 19) thus — *yaśasi dhavalatā varṇyate bāsa-kīrttyoh.* Verse 6 contains description relating to Skandagupta's conquests over his rivals and herein his comparison to Kṛṣṇa [*hatari pur iva kṛsṇaḥ*] is a good sample of simile. As an example of *virodhābhāsa,* we may cite the line — *notsikto na ca vismitaḥ pratidinaṁ samvardhamānadyutiḥ* (verse 7). When the poet narrates that the sound of Skandagupta's approaching arrows on the enemies is, as it were, the roaring of the river Gaṅgā [*lakṣyata iva strotreṣu gāṅgadhvaniḥ*— verse 8], we can instantly recognise it as an appropriate illustration of *uppreksā.*

Considering all these facts, it may be concluded that in this inscription there are the poet's sincere efforts to show an advancement as well as refinement towards poetic perfection; but at the same time we must admit that the poet lacks the requisite descriptive power, because, this inscription does not give a complete picture of any person or object. Skandagupta's battle with the *Hūṇas* (verse 8) was, perhaps, poetised in *raudra* sentiment, but unfortunately this portion is badly damaged. Ungrammatical forms, irregularities in Sandhi and spellings are lesser and insignificant here.

In the Junāgaḍh (in Gujarat) rock inscription of Skandagupta,[18] there are altogether forty-seven verses and the metres, used here, are *mālinī*, *āryā*, *upajāti*, *indravajrā*, *ardhasamamālabhāriṇī* (verse 16), *vaṁśastha* and *vasantatilaka*. This work bearing the dates 454, 450 and 457 A.D., was written a few years before the composition of the Mandasor inscription of Vatsabhaṭṭi. While Vatsabhaṭṭi's *praśasti* does concern with the descriptions, mainly, of the cities, oceans, mountains, seasons, etc., the present inscription favours to delineate the subtle characteristics of human mind. Of course, the picture of the Sudarśana lake depicted in this inscription, cannot be undervalued with apathetic outlook. It must be admitted that the inscription, as a whole, is not a good poetic creation, but there are some expressions which are akin to those of an efficient poet. We find a fine illustration of *rūpaka,* when Skandagupta's enemies are compared to serpants lifting up their hoods in pride and arrogance, viz., *narapati-bhujagānāṁ māna-darpot-phaṇānām* (verse 2). When the poet narrates that after his father had acquired the friendship of the gods (i.e. after his death), Skandagupta "cowed down his enemies and made subject to himself the whole earth, bounded by the water of the four oceans and full of thriving countries round the borders of it" (verse 3), we can distinguish this verse as an apt illustration of *atiśayokti.* the rivers' union with their husband i.e. ocean [*samudrakāntāś cirabandhanojjhitāḥ punaḥ patiṁ śāstra-yathocitaṁ yayuḥ* / / verse 28] is an excellent instance of *samāsokti.* Again, a good example of *virodhābhāsa* is traceable in the expression — *apīha loke sakale sudarśanam . . . . durdarśanatāṁ gataṁ kṣaṇāt* (verse 31). the expressions like — *sa jayati vijitārttir viṣṇur atyantajiṣṇuḥ* (verse 1), *lakṣmīḥ svayaṁ yaṁ varayāṁcakāra* (verse 5), *nṛṇām śaraṇyaḥ śaraṇāgatānām* (verse 15), *vavarṣa toyaṁ bahu saṁtataṁ ciram* (verse 29), etc., are certainly evidences of polished poetry and they bear likeness to beautiful poetic expressions invented by poets like Kālidāsa. The grammatical peculiarities in the usages, such as, *saṁraṁjayāṁ ca prakṛtīr babhūva* (verse 23) and *vicintayāṁ cāpi babhūvur utsukāḥ* (verse 30) can also be traced in the works of later classical poets. Again, the verse —

> *tasyātma jo hyātma jabhāvayukto*
> *dvidheva cātmātmavaśena nītaḥ /*
> *sarvātmanātmeva ca rakṣaṇīyo*
> *nityātmavān ātma jakāntarūpaḥ / /* (verse 14)

— is a fine illustration of alliteration and this type is not very common even in the renowned inscriptional writings.

This inscription evinces that during the middle of the 5th century A.D., there was a deep inclination towards bringing out lengthy and metrical epigraphical compositions. The style here is *Vaidarbhī*, but that of *Gauḍī* is also detectable. The poet uses harsh sounds like *niryantraṇānyonyagṛhapraveśaiḥ* (verse 23). The harsh and gorgeous words, while applied in a poetry, are designated by Daṇḍin (Kāvyādarśa, I. 72) as *dīptaguṇa* which is opposite to *saukumārya*.

The Eran (in Madhya Pradesh) stone pillar inscription of the time of Budhagupta,[19] dated 484 A.D., begins with three verses in *āryā* metre, which are followed by five prose lines. So, it may be considered a *campū* type of composition. The remarkable feature to be noted in this inscription is that the poet has a predilection for using alliteration; the play upon words which he often demonstrates, constitutes a popular feature in the later Sanskrit artificial prose works. When the poet uses the expression like — *sthityutpatti-nyayādihetur garuḍaketuḥ (line I)* he evidently tries to exhibit his expertise in literary adornment. The prose-portion, though it lacks the wealth of descriptions, contains features of ornamental style. The constructions like — *piturguṇānukāriṇo varuṇaviṣṇoḥ* (line 5), *putreṇātyanta-bhagavadbhaktena* (line 6) and *śatrusamara-jiṣṇunā mahārāja-mātṛviṣṇu* (line 7) — bring forth real rhythmic effects. A notable specimen of pun is given in the sentence — *puṇya-janārddanasya janārddanasya dhvajastambho'bhyucchritaḥ* (line 9).

Here, the word *puṇa janārddana* means "troubler of the demons", *puṇyajana* denoting a class of demons.

This inscription does not show special liking for lengthy compound forms and is free, to some extent, from the Prākṛt influence on spelling disorder; in most cases, it conforms to the Sandhi-rules. The author has not fully shown his perfection in utilising the *arthālaṁkāra*-s, but indication of his ability, in this regard, is not totally absent.

The Mandasor stone inscription of the time of Prabhākara,[20] dated 467 A.D., like other inscriptions found at the same locality, bears some excellent poetic specimens. Among the figures of speech illustrated in this record, remarkable are — *guptānvayavyoma (rūpaka)* and *Candrakalpaḥ śrī-Candraguptaḥ (Upamā)* in verse 2; *bhuvaḥpatīnāṁ bhuvi bhūpatitvam (anuprāsa)* in verse 3; *yamaka* on the word *govinda* in verse 4 and *senā* in verse 6; *yaśaśca yaś candramarīci-gauram (luptopamā)* in verse 7; alliteration with the letters *da, dha* and *ra (dadhāra dhārādhara-dhīra-ghoṣaḥ)* in verse 7; *bhūbhṛt-kula-candrikā (rūpaka)* in verse 8; *guptānvayāri-druma (rūpaka)* in verse 10; *yamaka* on the word *priyāsu* in verse 14; and *sarid aṅganā (rūpaka)* in verse 17. A fine illustration of *ullekha alaṁkāra* is—

dīne dhaneśaṁ dhiyi vāci ceśaṁ
ratau smaraṁ saṁyati pāśapāvṇīm /
yam arthi-vidvat-pramadāri-vargāḥ
sambhāvayañcakrur anekadhaikam // (v. 9)

A good simile has been illustrated when the qualities of the water contained in the *kūpa* are specified —

mano munīnām iva nirmalaṁ ca /
vaco gurūṇām iva cāmbu pathyam (v. 12)

Verses 14 and 15 are examples of charming poetic pieces where spring season with all its glory is delineated. These two verses, along with other stray poetic embellishments are enough to prove that the present inscription is the creation of a really good poet whose name is given as Ravila. Unfortunately no complete work or other short works of this poet, nay, of any inscriptional author have come down to us and due to this reason his real estimation as a poet cannot be properly done.

The Eran stone boar inscription of the time of Toramāṇa[21] (500-515 A.D.), bears evidence of the author's fondness of alliteration which occurs in several places. Thus, *ghana-ghoṇāghātaghūrṇita* (line 1), *pitur guṇānukāriṇo varuṇaviṣṇoḥ* (line 4), *aneka - śatru-samara-jiṣṇoḥ mahārāja-mātṛviṣṇoḥ* (line 5), *jagat-parāyanasya nārāyaṇasya* (line 7) are fine specimens of well-planned alliterations. The expression — *svayamvarayeva rājalakṣmyādhigatasya* (line 5) — where the goddess of sovereignty has been compared with a maiden, desirous of having the king as her husband, is an apt example of simile. This expression also appears in the Eran inscription of the time of Budhagupta. In the opening verse, Viṣṇu has been mentioned as the pillar for the support to the great house which is the three worlds [*trailokya-mahāgṛha-stambhaḥ*]. Here the superimposition of *nagara* on *trailokya*, and that of *mahāgṛhastambha* on Viṣṇu are fine illustrations of metaphor [*rūpaka*]; this is an example of *paramparita rūpaka* which has been defined by Viśvanatha as the superimposition of something upon another being the cause of another superimposition — *yatra kaśyacid āropaḥ parāropaṇakāraṇaṁ tat paramparitam / Sāhityadarpaṇa, X).* Similar invocation, addressed to Śiva, such as "the foundation pillar for the erection of the city which is the three worlds" may be found in the Aihole inscription of Śaka-saṁvat 1091[22] and also in Bāṇabhaṭṭa's *Harṣacarita* (Introductory verse I) where Śiva is described as — *trailokyanagarārambha-mūlastambha*.

The Mandasor inscription of Yaśodharman and Viṣṇuvardhana,[23] dated 532 A.D. and composed of thirty-two verses, is a fine poetic piece embedded with illustrations of innumerable *śabdālaṁkāra*-s and occasionally inserted *arthālaṁkāra*-s. Some of the examples of alliteration are — *sa jayati jagatāṁ patiḥ pinākī* (verse 1); *sṛjatu bhavasṛjo vaḥ kleśa-bhaṅgaṁ bhujaṅgaḥ* (verse 3); *atha jayati janendraḥ śrī-yaśodharmanāmā (verse 5) taruṇa-tarulatāvad vīrakvṛttiḥ* (verse 5); *ājau jitī vijayate jagatīm* (verse 6); *rājanvanto ramanto bhuja-vijita-*

bhuvā bhūrayo yena deśā (verse 8); *revā-vāri-rājiḥ* (verse 11); *sutaḥprasūto yaśasāṁ prasūtiḥ* (verse 12); *vibhratā śubhram abhraṁśi smārttaṁ vartmocitaṁ* (verse 14); *uditatarāgaṁ gīyate gīrabhijñaḥ* (verse 17) and so on. Attempt to illustrate *yamaka* may be found in the expressions like *vidura iva vidūraṁ prekṣayā prekṣamānaḥ* (verse 17); *ravir iva ravikīrttiḥ* (verse 13); *dharmato-dharma-doīaḥ* (verse 20]; *kṛta eva kṛtam etad* (verse 20); *upahita-hita-rakṣa* (verse 22), etc.

Of the *arthālaṁkāra-s, upamā* has been profusely illustrated. For example, Bhānuguptā is said to have given birth to three sons, as if, she had produced three sacrificial fires [*havir-bhuja ivādhvarān . . . tanayāṁstrīn a jījanat* — verse 15].

While describing Abhayadatta's death, he is said to have been cut off by the mighty Yama, just as a tree is uprooted by a lordly elephant (verse 23), and this is undoubtedly a fine illustration of simile. *Utprekṣā* and *samāsokti* are illustrated in the expression that the songs of cuckoos cleave open, as it were, the mids of those who are far away from their beloved [*kokilānāṁ pralāpā bhindantīva . . . proṣitānāṁ manāṁsi* — verse 25]; these two figures of speech are to be seen again when the ocean is described as embracing the orb of the moon with its lofty waves, as if with long arms (verse 27). Similar figures of speech are also found exemplified here and there.

Allusions to the sixty thousand sons of Sāgara digging out the ocean (verse 4), to Uddhava supporting the Andhakas (verse 6) and to Vidhura, the younger brother of Dhṛtarāṣṭra, who, on account of his insight, could look far ahead — certainly add to the literary weight of the inscriptions.

The verses of this inscription are ornate and display artistic beauty. Some passages remind us of the finished creation of a gifted poet. Thus, verses 25-27 describe in an excellent manner the spring season when the well was excavated. These are good examples of the poet's commendable efficiency in showing his imaginative aptness.

All the popular metres have been efficiently employed. These are *āryā* (verse 24); *indravajrā* (verse 10); *upajāti* (verses 4 and 12); *puṣpitāgrā* (verse 1); *mandākrantā* (verse 25); *mālinī* (it seems to be the poet's most favourite metre, for, it is used in ten verses, viz., 3, 5, 11, 13, 17, 18, 20, 21, 22 and 26); *vasantatilaka* (verses 6 and 7); *śādūlavikrīḍita* (verse 9); *śālinī* (verse 28); *śikhariṇī* (verses 2 and 23); *śloka* (verses 14, 15 and 16); and *sragdharā* (verses 8, 19 and and 27).

Another remarkable literary inscription is the Gwalior stone inscription of Mihirakula[24] (515-545 A.D.). It was composed of thirteen verses by one Keśava, no other work of whom is known for certain. His poetic talent, however, as reflected in the well-planned and beautifully textured verses, is certainly to be appreciated; the metres used in this record are *āryā, mālinī* and *śārdūlavikrīḍita.* like a gifted poet, he has invoked the Sun gold in the two opening verses. The description of the month of Kārtika (verse 6) and the concluding verse where prayer is made for long endurance of the Sun temple are speciments of good poetry, having choices words and senses. Some of the figures of speech, illustrated in this record, are marks of the style of not an ordinary poet. Thus, in *bhuvana-bhavana-dīpaḥ* (verse 2), *nṛpavṛṣa* (verse 5) and *śaśiraśmi-hāsaḥ* (verse 6) we find appropriate examples of *rūpaka,* and in the expression *tapita-kanaka-varṇair aṁśubhiḥ paṇka jānām abhinava-ramaṇīyaṁ yo vidhatte* (verse 2), an appreciable illustration of *pariṇāma* may be detected.

Thus the inscriptions, discussed above, possess immense literary significance and have achieved ornate poetic exuberance. The sytle and diction of these inscriptions evince that they were produced by men not widely known, but of high poetic calibre. If the entire Gupta inscriptions are taken into consideration, it becomes evident that a wide cultivation of poetry, both in prose and verse, was processed through the inscriptional writings. Inscriptions written in prose, verse and mixed language showed their versatile excellence during the period under review. In regard to versification, these inscriptions, in spite of several of their excellent ornamental verses, have not found a rightful place in the vast region of Sanskrit poetry; in reality, Sanskrit metrical writing originated in a far-off period and attained sufficient progress and development already before the emergence of the Gupta power. The inscriptional verses, therefore, could not add fresh technicalities to the poetic world that had already accomplished maturity. The verses, in many cases, have been influenced by earlier or contemporaneous poetic creations. In the field of prose compositions, the inscriptions have no notable predecessor. As it has been pointed out earlier, the inscriptions, written in prose, were instrumental to bringing out later elevated prose compositions which achieved complete success in the works of Bāṇabhaṭṭa, Subandhu and Daṇḍin. Prose has been held by Sanskrit rhetoricians as the touchstone for estimating the poetic ability of a scholar.[25] The epigraphical literature including the compositions like Junagaḍh inscription of Rudradāman and Allahabad *praśasti* of Samudragupta may be considered to be superior to extant Sanskrit prose literature excepting, of course, the works of Bāṇabhaṭṭa, Subandhu and Daṇḍin. A major protion of the inscriptions, especially the land-grants, is in prose, the invocatory portion at the beginning and the benedictory and the imprecatory portions at the conclusion being a verses. But the mixture of prose and verse was a favourite device of the authors of the inscriptions. The elaborate prose and metrical writings in these inscriptions establish that the writers of these *praśastis* conform to the rules of *alaṁkāra*, made into defintie shape later on in the treatises of Bhāmaha, Daṇḍin and Visśvanātha.

NOTES AND REFERENCES

1. *Epigraphia Indica,* Vol. VIII, pp. 42f.
2. J. F. Fleet, *Corpus Inscriptionum Indicarum (C.I.I.),* Vol. III, Varanasi, 1970, No. 1, pp. 1ff.
3. G. Bühler, "The Indian Inscriptions and the Antiquity of Indian Artificial Poetry". *Indian Antiquary,* Vol. XLII, 1913. p. 172.
4. cf. *gadyapadyamayaṁ kāvyaṁ camūr ityabhidīyate* / *Sāhityadarpana,* VI, 312.
5. cf. *gadyapadyamayī rājastutir birudam ucyate, ibid.,* VI, 313.
6. *I.A.,* XLII, p. 176.
7. Keith, *Hisotry of Sanskrit Literature,* Oxford, 1956, p. 78.
8. *ojaḥ samāsabhūyastvam etad gadyasya jīvitam* — Kāvyādarśa, I, 80.
9. Keith, History of Sanskrit Literature, p. 78.
10. *padye'pyadākṣiṇātyānām idam ekam pārāyanam* / — Kāvyādarśa, I, p. 80.
11. *I.A. XLII,* p. 179.
12. *Ep. Ind.,* XXI, pp. 8f.
13. *C.I.I.,* III, No. 6. pp 35f.

13* *C.I.I.*, III, pp. 31f.
14. *C.I.I.*, Vol. III, pp. 43f.
15. *C.I.I.*, Vol. 17, pp. 74f.
16. *C.I.I.*, Vol. III, No. 18, pp. 79f.
17. *C.I.I.*, Vol. III, pp. 53f.
18. D.C. Sircar, *Select Inscriptions*, Calcutta, 1965, pp. 307f.
19. *Ibid.*, 334f.
20. *Ep. Ind.*, Vol. XXVII, pp. 12f.
21. *C.I.I.*, Vol. III, pp. 159f.
22. *Indian Antiquary*, Vol. IX, p. 97.
23. *C.I.I.*, Vol. III, pp. 150f.
24. *C.I.I.*, Vol. III, pp. 161f.
25. *gadyaṁ kavīnāṁ nikasaṁ vadanti* — Vāmana's Kāvyālaṁkāra-sūtra, 1.3.21.

13

Surgical Profession in Ancient India

K. KRISHNAMURTHY

The medical profession with special reference to the surgical profession as it existed thousands of years ago in ancient India will be briefly presented in the following article. The material presented here is based on the works of several distinguished scholars to whom this writer is greatly indebted.

Frequently it is customary to label the ancient past as having been "primitive" in knowledge as compared to modern times. The available literature on the medical sciences in ancient India, however, reveals that the knowledge was "advanced" and some of it even was astonishing. A note of caution is also necessary. One must be very careful in interpreting the various descriptions in the ancient literature to avoid the inevitable pitfalls of misinterpretation. Many of the works in the ancient literature cannot be dated with any degree of precision. No attempt will be made here to present a chronological description. The material discussed in this article will cover a period of several centuries.

The Beginning

Dhanvantarī is considered to be the father of the ancient Hindu medicine. He had the following disciples : Aupadhenva, Aurobhara, Gopuraksata, Bhoja, Pousakalvanta and Suśruta. The last two disciples wrote treatise on the Practice of Surgery. Only Suśruta's work which appears to have been edited subsequently by several anonymous authors, appears to have existed. The exact period of Suśruta's existence is unknown but is believed to be earlier to 600 B.C.F.

Medical Education

Several universities (institutions of higher education) had existed in the ancient era and the well known among them were Nālandā University had a student population of 8,500, a faculty of 1,510 (faculty to student ratio being 1 : 6) and a supporting staff of 2,000. There were students from far away countries such as China, Java and Ceylon (Sri Lanka). The income, generated from the several villages endowed to the University by the King, supported the University.

The medical education consisted of six years of study. Students had to be at least of sixteen years of age and had to meet rigorous admission requirements. At the time of graduation, the students were graded into following ranks :

Buddhi-yuta (Intelligent)
Madhyama Buddhi-yuta (Moderately Intelligent)
Alpa-Buddhi-yuta (Less Intelligent)

Making of a Surgeon

Suśruta is the father of the surgical profession of ancient India. His treatise describes in details about the surgical profession and procedures.

After graduation, surgical training was obtained under a preceptor, a well known teacher of his time. Training consisted of observing and assisting the teacher. The practical knowledge was gained not only through assisting the teacher but also practicing on inanimate objects such as gourds, leather bags and dried fruits. Suśruta insisted on medical conferences to exchange ideas. He placed great emphasis on both didactic and practical training for the surgeons. This is quite evident in the following quotation : "He who is only trained in theory but not experienced in practical knowledge, knows not what he should do when treating a patient but behaves foolishly like a youth on a battle field;

on the other hand a physician who is educated in practical knowledge but not in theory will not earn the respect of wise men."

After several years of rigorous training and upon the favourable recommendation of the preceptor, a candidate was permitted to apply to the King to obtain a license to practice surgery. As a part of the professional ethics, surgeons were required to possess a keen sense of observation, to maintain an uprighteous conduct, to have pleasant speech and manners, to be friendly with all living beings and not to associate with quacks.

Surgical Procedures

Analgesia for surgical procedures appears to have been practiced. Usually analgesia was obtained with the use of wine mixed with unidentified herbs. Burning of Indian hemp (cannabis indica) was also apparently used for analgesic purposes. Significantly however there is no mention of the use of any opium or its products.

General descriptions for preparation to perform surgical procedures include the washing of hands, trimming the nails and fumigating the operating area with burning of benzoin (a resin). References are also made to clean the operating area.

Surgical instruments, in great numbers, were in use and a detailed description of them is available in the treatise by Suśruta.

The wounds were treated with caustics (Kṣāra), cauterised with fire (Agni) and various oils (Kalka) were applied to them. To aid in wound healing, wounds were irrigated with oil, honey and buttermilk. The bandages were made of dried leaves (Patta) and cotton. Load stone (Magnet) was used to locate and extract metallic foreign bodies. Suture material consisted of twine, horse's hair and silkworm gut. The technique of suturing consisted of continuous, interrupted, grilled or twisted sutures.

Some degree of specialization appears to have existed. Jīvaka (a contemporary of the Buddha) was practicing mostly paediatrics and Nimi was said to have practiced ophthalmology.

Some of the surgical procedures described in the treatise by Suśruta, were unknown to ancient Greeks. Laprotomies (opening of the abdominal cavity) were done for foreign bodies, injuries and other conditions such as volvulus reveals that exposed intestines were covered with honey after untwisting and prior to replacing them into the abdominal cavity. Paracentesis was frequently performed to remove fluid from abdomen in cases of ascites. Growths from various parts of the body were excised. Trocar aspiration of hydroceles and surgery for removal of bladder stones were also practiced. Ear lobe reconstruction, rhinoplasty and skin grafting techniques have been described in detail. Cataract extraction, caesarian section as well as intra-uterine fetal destruction were also practiced. There are also descriptions of amputation of limbs as well as fitting of amputees with artifical wooden legs.

Cranial Surgery

Anatomy and function of the nervous system was vaguely understood. Nevertheless, several statements are found in the literature that are fascinating. Suśruta states that "Head (brain) is the center of senses; head (brain) is the only organ that makes function of all other organs in the body possible," Bhela states that "head (brain) is the center of mind."

Jīvaka was said to have done cranial surgery. From the description it is not clear whether the procedure was indeed an intracranial procedure. However, the surgery done on King Bhoja (627 A.D.), appears to have been an intracranial procedure for the removal of tumor.

Philosophy of Medicine

A very concise statement by Caraka clearly depicts the philosophical concept of the art of healing. He stated "Na jagati ana-auṣadhan" (which roughly translated means that there is nothing in this world that cannot be used as medicine.) The art of healing does not merely involve administration of medications and/or surgical intervention. This statements by Caraka is ageless and is true for today as well.

NOTES AND REFERENCES

1. *An Interpretation of Ancient Hindu Medicine* (1922), by C. Chakrabarty, Calcutta; Nerraj Publishing House (1983).
2. *The Antiquity of Hindu Medicine* (1930), by D. Choury Muthu, (1930 3rd edition) London; Bailliere, Tindall & Cox.
3. *Charaka Samhita V* (1949), Edited by Shree Gulabkunveda Ayurvedic Society, Jamnager; Gulabkunverba Ayurvedic Society.
4. *Medicine and Pharmacy in India* (1964). by Dr. P. K. Sanyal, Calcutta; A. Mukherjee & Co.
5. *Ancient Indian Medicine by Dr. Kutumbaiah* (1962) Bombay; Orient Longmans.
6. *Text Book of Ayurveda* (1946) by Dr. Laxmipathi Bezwada, India, A. Laxmipathi.
7. *The Culture and Civilization of Ancient India* (1970) by D. D. Kosambi, Delhi; Vikas Publications.
8. *Science and Secrets of Early Medicine* (1962) by Jurgenthurwald, translated by Richard and Clara Winston London; Thames & Hudson.

be used as medicine). The art of healing does not merely involve administration of medicaments and surgical intervention. This statement by Charaka is ageless and is true for today as well.

NOTES AND REFERENCES

1. An Interpretation of Ancient Hindu Medicine (1922) by C. Chakraberty, Calcutta: [illegible] Publishing House (1951).
2. The Antiquity of Hindu Medicine (1930) by D. Chowdhury, Madras (19[illegible] 3rd edition; London: Baillière, Tindall & Cox.
3. Charaka Samhita (1949). Edited by Shree Gulab Kunverba Ayurvedic Society, Jamnagar: Gulab Kunverba Ayurvedic Society.
4. Medicine and Pharmacy in India (1964) by Dr. P. K. Sen, Calcutta: Mukhopadhyay & Co.
5. Ancient Indian Medicine by P. Kutumbiah (1962) Bombay: Orient Longmans.
6. Text Book of Ayurveda (1949) by Dr. [illegible], India: R. Laxmanan.
7. The Culture and Civilisation of Ancient India (1970) by D. D. Kosambi, Delhi: Vikas Publications.
8. Science and Secrets of Early Medicine (1962) by Jürgen Thorwald, translated by Richard and Clara Winston. London: Thames & Hudson.

14

Development of Medicine in Ancient India

OM P. SHARMA

I. The Origin

The history of medicine in Ancient India takes us back to remote antiquity. Medicine in India can be safely divided into three phases *(Fig. 1)*.

A. Prevedic : Medicine of Prehistoric India : The Pre-Vedic era extends from the earliest times to the Aryan invasion of India in about 1500 B.C. This was the time of magical or magico-religious phenomena which were atttributed to supernatural causes. The diseases were treated by magic, incantations, charms, amulets and talismans. The excavations of Mohenjo-daro and Harappa in Indus Valley tell us that the then prevailing civilization was contemporary with Mesopotamia, Egypt and Crete and that they communicated with each other and shared their views on religious and medical matters. The Indus valley civilization existed as long as 5000 years B.C. The excavations depict a highly developed life with broad streets, well constructed houses made of well burnt bricks. Hygienic principles were followed; houses were ventilated and lighted. Houses had wells, drains and bathrooms. Indeed, the most imposing structure at Mohenjo-daro is the Great Bath.

B. Vedic Medicine : Our knowledge of Vedic Medicine is derived from two Vedas, the Ṛg-Veda and the Atharva-Veda. Vedic medicine believed, that diseases were caused by possession of evil spirit, by demons and sorcerers, and ghosts and goblins. The medicine then was an amalgam of religion, magic and empirico-rational elements. The medicine of the Atharva-Veda is the science of the primitive man who regards everything he cannot explain as the work of a god. He is ever ready to see in any disease the manifestation of a supernatural power. Some diseases are attributed to the greater gods, and this often as a punishment for sin. Varuna sends dropsy *(Jalodara)* as a punishment for sin. Certain sharp pains are ascribed to the spear of Rudra. Agni is regarded as producing fever, headache, and cough. Vedic medicine thus believed that diseases were caused by possession of evil spirits, anger of certain gods, by evil deeds, and the sorcery of enemies. This is the reason why Atharva-veda deals with the treatment by making offerings, oblations, penances, fasting, incantations and purificatory rites. The main diseases which occur in Vedic medical texts include, fever, cough, diarrhea, consumption, dropsy, tumor, leprosy and skin diseases, inherited diseases and seizures by demons. In the Atharva-Veda itself only a few medicines are mentioned. There are only a few practices of real therapeutic value : the most delicate is the probing of the urethra, which seems to be described in XXV. 15.16, for the relief from retention of urine; the giving of an enema as a substitute for operation; the application of leaches to sores is found in XXX. 16. ; the application of a torch to the serpent bite.

C. Post-Vedic period : The post-Vedic period extends from 800 B.C. to 200 A.D. This period is divisible into two periods : the first extending from the completion of the collection of Vedic hymns (800 B.C.) to the rise of medical schools (600 B.C.); the second from the rise of medical schools to the end of classical Indian Medicine. The age of Brāhmanas and the Upaniṣads (800-600 B.C.) was an epoch of great intellectual ferment and spiritual revolt. New faiths viz., Buddhism, Jainism had arisen. Āyurveda developed as an upānga or upaveda of Atharva-veda. Āyurveda consisted of eight divisions but only one of the eight divisions dealt with demonism. The medicine now no longer was magico-religious but become empirico-rational. Tradititon teaches the beginning of medicine to be mythical. Indra taught the science of medicine to Ātreya and the science of surgery to Dhanvantarī. This indicates that Ātreya the physician, and Suśruta, the surgeon were the first founder of their respective departments of medicine and science. At the time of the Buddha, there existed two great universities. Texila or Takṣaśīlā in the West and Kāśī or Benares in the East. These two great schools graduated many famous students who write treatises on medicine and surgery. These books (tantras) constitute earliest medical literature and formed the bases of teachings in medical schools. We have three important Saṃhitās : the Caraka; Suśruta, and Bhela (Fig. 2)

II. The Manuscripts

A. **The Caraka Saṃhitā** stands as the finest document of the creative period (600 B.C. — 200 A.D.). This massive treatise on ancient Indian medicine contains eight divisions. Each division is further divided into numerous chapters. It describes not only the existing knowledge about medicine in all aspects but also the logic and philosophy behind the system. When did Caraka, the creator of Caraka Saṃhitā live is not known with any centainty. Some historians believe that Caraka lived before Pāṇini, the grammarian, who is said to have lived before sixth century B.C. Another theory postulates that Caraka is identical with Patañjali, who is also said to have expounded the science of yoga. Patañjali lived around 175 B.C. and wrote a commentary on the medical work of Caraka. Then, Caraka must have lived sometime before him. Sylvan Levi believes that Caraka was a court physician to the Indo-Scythian King Kaniṣka. It seems Caraka lived between the seventh, eighth and ninth centuries when Arabic scholarship was at its height. Caraka was a revered authority in the Saracen and Latin World of medicine.

Caraka Saṃhitā deals with fetal generation and development, anatomy of the human body, function and malfunction of the body depending upon the equilibrium of the three humours of the body; vāyu, pitta, kapha. It describes etiology, classification, pathology and diagnosis, prognosis, treatment and the science of rejuvenation. It discusses the basis of Tridoṣa theory. We also find detailed description of many ocular diseases, the female genital organs, normal and abnormal deliveries and children. Materia-medica consists of about 50 groups of drugs acting on various system.

B. Suśruta Saṃhitā is the main source of knowledge about surgery in India. Suśruta taught his surgical techniques first on dummies and later on dead bodies. His techniques of dissecting human body were novel and innovative. His operations for constructing a new nose or ear lobe, lithotomy and abdominal operations, and taking out dead fetus are classics. Saśruta Saṃhitā was translated into Arabic before the end of the eighth century A.D. It was translated into Latin by Hassler, and into German by Ullers. It was translated into English by Hoernle (1897) and K.L. Bhisagaratna (1917).

C. Kāśyapa Saṃhitā deals with diseases of children. This was enunciated by sage Mārica Kāśyapa. A redaction of it was performed during the Gupta period.

D. Bower Manuscript : This very important manuscript was discovered by a man of Kuchar in February 1980. Kuchar is an oasis of Eastern Turkestan in Central Asia on the caravan route of China. This route was used by the Buddhist monks of India travelling to far off places. The manuscript was bought for a small sum by L. H. Bower. It was deciphered and published by Hoernle who spent twenty years on its study. On palaeographic evidence, the manuscript is dated between 350 and 370 A.D. The importance of Bower manuscript (Navanitaka) as a source book for ancient Indian medicine is tremendous. It confirms the existence of the Caraka Saṃhitā, Suśruta Saṃhitā, Bhela Saṃhitā, and the Uttaratantra. The Bower manuscript was sold to Bodlein Library in Oxford.

III. Universities in Ancient India

In ancient India, one could become a physician by selecting a proper preceptor, and presenting himself to him. He could go to *gurukula* where the students lived with the teachers. These *gurukulas* were located outside the cities, in the forests. Students also could join one of the many medical universities in the larger cities. The following three universities were famous.

A. Nālandā : Nālandā was the largest residential university India ever had. It had a population of 8,500 pupils and 1,510 teachers. There were many executives and workers; the total population was about 12,000. The method of instruction was individual and small group discussions. The ruins of the ancient University of Nālandā are situated in Bihar near the village of Baragaon, 65 miles southeast of Patna. The area covered by Nālandā was a mile long and half a mile broad. It was enclosed by a high wall all around it. The buildings were planned. There were eight big halls and 300 lecture rooms. Boarding and lodging were free for students. The best account of Nālandā University is that given by two Chinese pilgrims, Hiuen Tsang (Yuan Chwang) and I-Tsing who came to India during the reign of emperor Harśa. They both spent many years at Nālandā as students. To be a student at Nālandā was the highest distinction of the day. Nālandā flourished from the fifth to the twelfth century A.D. The students came there from China, Korea, Tibet, Mongolia and Japan.

B. Taxila (Takṣaśīlā) : Dating from the sixth century B.C., Taxila was the most important seat of learning in ancient India. It attracted students from all corners of India, and abroad. The location of Taxila was on the great trade route between India and Central Asia. Pliny calls it a famous city; Strabo declares it as a large city; Arrean describes it as a great and flourishing city. Some of the most learned men in ancient India were said to have been educated at Taxila : Ātreya, Canakya (Kauṭilya), Pāṇini, Jīvaka, Vyāḍi, Nāgārjuna, Brāhmadatta and other.

The remains of Taxila are situated about twenty miles northwest of Rawalpindi in Punjab (now in Pakistan).

C. Kāśī (Benares) : Kāśī University was organised on the lines of Taxila University by many of the students from Taxila. It flourished from the 7th century B.C. to 12th century A.D. The School of Surgery was the most attractive feature of Benares University.

IV. Medical Education and Ethics

A. Selection of the student : A great deal of importance was attached to moral fitness, for moral excellence was the basis of all true education. It was understood that before the student was admitted, he had to undergo a period of probation for six months to one year. Preference was given to the member of families with long medical traditions to enter the medical professions.

B. Initiation or Upanayana Ceremony : Having been accepted, the student was initiated into a special ceremony — Upanayana ceremony. Each had its own version of the Oath of Initiation. The following are the only few Caraka Saṃhitā:

> "Thou shalt lead the life of the bachelor (brahmacārin), grow beard and hair, speak only the truth, eat not meat, eat only pure articles of food, be free from envy and carry no arms."

> "Thou shalt delicate thyself to me and regard me as thy chief. . . . . Acting either at my behest or otherwise, thou shalt conduct thyself for achievement of thy teacher's purpose along, the best of thy abilities."

> "No offering of gifts by a woman without the behest of her husband or guardian shall be accepted by thee . . . . ."

> "The peculiar customs of the patient's household shall not be made public. Even knowing that the patient's span of life has come to its close, it shall not be mentioned by thee there, where if done so, it would cause shock to the patients or to others."

> "Though possessed of knowledge, one should not boast very much of one's knowledge. Most people are offended by the boastfulness of even those, who are otherwise good and authoritative."

Medical education was pursued with a spirit of dedication, as is evidenced by the Oath of Initiation. The student was made clearly aware of how he should behave as a student and as a physician. Practical training of a medical student had three objectives : (1) preparation of medicines; (2) training in surgery; and (3) examination of patients. The student learnt the art of preparing flower juices, intoxicating liquors, herbal combinations, combination of mineral and herbs. Incisions were taught by making cuts on gourds, watermelon, cucumber; suturning was taught on pieces of skin, hide or cloth; bandaging or ligaturing by tying bandages round the limbs and on a full-sized doll; cauterizing was demonstrated on a piece of soft flesh; and the art of giving ememas by asking a student to insert a tube into the mouth of a gourd. Equal importance was given to theoretical and practical training. "One without the other results in an inexpert, confused, and half-baked intellectual. They are like one-winged birds."

C. The Convocation or Samāvartana Ceremony : After the conclusion of studies, when the young physician was about to embark on his medical career the ceremony of Samāvartana was held. Again the student was asked to repeat the Oath of Initiation. Then they were charged about their future conduct and behaviour by the convocation Oath. Some parts of the Oath are given below:

> "Acting at my behest, thou halt conduct thyself for achievement of the teacher's purposes alone to the best of thy abilities."
>
> "Thou shouldst speak words that are gentle, pure, and righteous, pleasing, worthy, true, wholesome, and moderate. Thy behaviour must be in consideration of time and place and heedful of past experience. Thou shalt act always with a view to the acquisition of knowledge and the fullness of equipment."
>
> "There is no limit at all to the Science of Life (Āyurveda) : So thou shalt apply thyself to it with diligence. This is how thou shouldst act. Again thou shouldst learn the skill of practice from another without carping. The entire world is the teacher to the intelligent and the foe to the unintelligent. Hence, know this well, thou shouldst listen and act according to the words of instruction of even an unfriendly person, when they are worthy and such as bring

fame to you and long life, and are capable of giving you strength and prosperity."

Suśruta Saṃhitā adds : "The twice born (Brahmin), the preceptor, the good and the destitute — these thou shalt treat, when they come to thee like thy own kith and kin and relieve their ailments with thy medications. Thus behaving good will befall thee. Thus thy learning will attain popularity and will gain for thee friends, fame, righteousness, wealth, and fulfilment."

D. Registration : After finishing the medical curriculum, one had to obtain the permission of the king to start one's professional carreer. "Having studied the Science, having fully grasped the meaning, having acquired practical skill and having performed operations on dummies, with ability to teach the science, and with the king's permission, a physician should enter into his profession."

V. Where was the Patient Treated ?

A. Clinics : It was customary to look after the patient in his own house but physicians also had their own clinics. These strong and spacious buildings were away from smoke, heat, dust, and undesirable noise, sight, and odour. Attendants were celan, affectionate and sympathetic. Commonly used medicines and remedies for emergency treatment were kept ready. There were special clinics for delivering babies, and postoperative units. All the clinics were designed by experts.

B. Hospitals : Hospitals for men and animals were established during the reign of Maurya and Gupta kings. Aśoka started many dispensaries not only in India but also in the surrounding countries. Buddhism gave a strong impetus to this movement. The following is from Aśoka's inscription — Rock Edict No. II (Girnar Text) :

> " . . . . Everywhere King Priyadarśī, beloved of the Gods, has arranged for two kinds of medical treatment : medical treatment for men and medical treatment for animals and, wherever there were

no medical herbs beneficial to men and animals, everywhere they have caused to be imported and planted. Wherever there were no roots and fruits, everywhere they have been caused to be dug and trees have been caused to be planted for the enjoyment of animals and men." — 274-236 B.C.

Fa-hien (A.D. 405-411) who visited India gives a description of the "*charitable dispensaries in Patliputra.*" He states: "The nobles and house holders of this country have founded hospitals within the city to which the poor of all countries, the destitute, the cripple, and the diseased may come. They receive every kind of help free and freely .... "

Hiuen Tsang (A.D. 629-645) came to India during the time of Harśa describes, "In all the highways of the town and villages, he (the emperor) erected 'hospices' (puṇya-śālas), provided with food and drink, and stationed there physicians with medicines for travellers and poor persons to be given without any stint."

Such institutions, either dispensaries or hospitals for the poor and the needy or poor houses equipped with medicines were found throughout India. These were the forerunners of the Western almhouses, monastries, and infirmaries.

VI. The Theory of Tridoṣa

Throughout Āyurveda the doctrine of tridoṣa plays an important role. It started from the term tri-dhātu (Ṛgveda 1.3.6) : The tridoṣa include *Vāyu* (Air); *Pitta* (bile); and *Kapha* (phlegm). These three doṣas control and regulate all the functions of the body. These doṣas are likely to be deranged by unsuitable food, adverse climate and other environmental factors, thus causing ill health and disease. Three doṣas are also affected by mental states. There is an increase of Vāyu in grief or worry; an increase of Pitta in anger or wrath; and an increase of Kapha in depression. Normal Vāyu is responsible for enthusiasm; normal pitta for intellect and memory and normal kapha is responsible for strength and courage. Thus here Āyurveda is concerned not only with bodily functions and physical health but also describes the relationship of the mind and the body. Inherited tendencies were explained, according to Caraka, by the transmigration of the soul from one life to another. Āyurveda recognizes undesirable emotions as disease and prescribes detachment and self control for their cure. Six undesirable emotions are: Kāma (sexual desire), Krodha (anger), Lobha (greed), Moha (infatuation), Mada (haughtiness) and Mātsarya (jealousy). This however means excess of these emotions was undesirable. Hence control is recommended.

VII. Classification of Diseases :

Indians classified various diseases according to their causes, severity of symptoms, the parts of the body involved, the pathology, and prognosis. Caraka divided the diseases into curable and incurable; mild and violent; of the mind and of the body; due to accidental causes and due to constituent elements; those arising from the stomach and those from the intestines.

Suśruta divides diseases into three main classes :

I. Physical :
- (a) hereditary : leprosy, piles
- (b) congenital : lameness, blindness
- (c) derangement of doṣas
  - * Bodily
  - * Mental

II. Disturbances in the physical environment of men
- (a) caused by weapons
- (b) caused by wild animals

III. Due to acts of God or nature
- (a) Seasonal type :
- (b) Providential type : thunder, lightning
- (c) Natural type : hunger, old age

VIII. Diagnosis

Caraka Saṃhitā describes only three methods of diagnosing a disease.

(1) Instruction of the inspired or the wise; (2) Observation, and (3) Inference. Suśruta added the fourth one i.e. interrogation. Bhavamisra improved upon these two classifications and expanded into eight steps; (1) Instruction by the wise, (2) observation, (3) inferance, (4) examination of the pulse, (5) examination of the eyes, (6) tongue, (7) voice, (8) urine, (Fig. 3).

IX. Prognosis

Prognosis was taught and learned very seriously. In ancient times, if a physician undertook to treat a patient that had a curable disease and the patient died, he not only lost prestige among his colleagues and people in general but also likely to be punished by the king. The surgeon was also required to inform the king beforehand of the seriousness and danger involved in the operation. The prognosis was assessed of the patient, (2) general constitution, (3) omens (4) dreams. (Fig. 4).

X. Treatment

(a) Medicines were derived from the vegetables, the animals (flesh, fat, bone marrow, tendons, horns, hoofs, hair, nails, skin, urine) and the earth (śilājeet, gold, silver, copper, lead, tin, iron, arsenic, antimony, precious stones). Caraka Saṃhitā classifies drugs into 50 categories, according to their use against different symptoms. Suśruta Saṃhitā classifies 400 drugs under 37 groups.

(b) Much importance was attributed to diet. Certain articles were considered incompatible e.g. fish and milk; uncooked meat and liver. Tonics were popular. Emetics and purgatives were prescribed to cleanse the system and restore youth, memory and vigour.

Drugs were administered by mouth, rectal enemas and vaginal pessaries, inhalations and fumigations. Caraka lists 13 different method of applying heat.

Conclusion

Ayurvedic medicine dates back to the time when Aryans came to India from Central Asia about 2000 yuears B.C. Even in the Pre-Vedic period, as indicated by the excavations of Mohenjo-daro and Harappa, hygiene and sanitation had reached a high degree of development. Why study Hindu Medicine at all ? Zimmer in his outstanding monograph wrote " . . . . . . the present work offers an approach to the understanding of the aims and ideals of Hindu medicine, its characteristics, and its possible value for stimulating and enlarging the view of today's medicine. Since the latter is, after all, confronted with the same questions as the physicians and sages of ancient and medieval India. Modern medicine may well gain a fresh impulse and insight through reviewing the venerable history of the Hindu discipline."